50 CHILDREN'S LITURGIES
for ALL OCCASIONS

D0898636

Sr. Joan Christie, OP

Please return to
teacher's lounge.

50 CHILDREN'S LITURGIES for all OCCASIONS

Francesca Kelly

XXIII
TWENTY-THIRD PUBLICATIONS
Mystic, Connecticut 06355

First Edition 1992 published by
THE COLUMBA PRESS
93 The Rise, Mount Merrion, Blackrock, Co Dublin

The author and publishers gratefully acknowledge the kind permission of Harper Collins to use extracts from *Listen* and *Praise*, both by A.J. McCallen; Oxford University Press for extracts from *New World: The Heart of the New Testament* by Alan Dale; Veritas Publications for an extract from *Walk in Love;* The National Christian Education Council for extracts from *It's Our Assembly.*

Twenty-Third Publications
185 Willow Street
P.O. Box 180
Mystic CT 06355
(203) 536-2611
800-321-0411

© Copyright 1992 Sister Francesca Kelly. All rights reserved. No part of this publication may be reproduced in any manner without prior written permission of the publisher. Write to Permissions Editor.

ISBN 0-89622-541-0
Library of Congress Catalog Card Number 92-82676

Contents

1. Celebrating Our Baptism

Today we recall our baptism. Then we were too small to know or remember. God called us and chose us to live as his children, in goodness and friendship. He gave us the Spirit of love to help us. Let us always be kind and loving children of God.

First Prayer
God our Father, you called us in baptism to be your children and to live like Jesus. Help us to answer your call and to live in the way of Jesus. We make this prayer through Jesus Christ, your Son, who lives and reigns with you in the unity of the Holy Spirit, one God forever and ever. Amen.

First Reading Titus 3:4-7
This reading comes from one of the letters of St. Paul. He is telling us that God wants us to be God's children and to be happy with God forever.

Dear Titus,
When we were baptized, we all became the children of God. This proves how good and kind God is because Godstill loved us even though we did not deserve it! When we were baptized, God gave us the Spirit of love to help us to be kind and loving as God is. This was done because God wanted us to be God's children and to be happy with God forever.
The Word of the Lord.

Responsorial Psalm Ephesians 1:3-6
God loves us because we are God's children. Let us praise and thank God.
RESPONSE: Let us praise God.
1. Give thanks to God the Father. God has made us brothers and sisters of Christ! R.
2. Even before the world was made, God chose us to be God's very own people—the people of Christ. R.

3. God wanted us to live like Jesus—in goodness and friendship, for God had decided that we should be God's own children. R.
4. Loving us so much, God wanted us to be God's sons and daughters. R.

Gospel Acclamation
Alleluia, alleluia.
God the Father said:
"You are my Son and I love you."
Alleluia.

Gospel Mark 1:9-11
The reading comes from the Gospel of St. Mark. It is the story of the baptism of Jesus, and it reminds us how much God the Father loves the Son.

One day, Jesus went to the river Jordan to see John the Baptist, and he asked John to baptize him in the river there. When Jesus came up out of the water he saw the Holy Spirit, who came to him like a dove from the sky, and God the Father said, "You are my Son and I love you."
The Gospel of the Lord.

Prayer of the Faithful
God our Father, you have called us to be your children and to live like Jesus. We pray that you will help us to do what you ask, and to live in the way of Jesus.
1. We pray that God will help our mothers and fathers, to make our homes, happy, loving places. Lord, hear us. R.
2. We pray that God will help all of us to make our parish a loving, caring place for the good of everyone. Lord, hear us. R.
3. We pray that God will help us to live and work well together in our school for the good of everyone. Lord, hear us. R.
4. We pray that God will help us to be friendly and loving, always ready to make u, when we have fights. Lord, hear us. R.

5. We pray that God will help us to be friends, and learn to understand each other. Lord, hear us. R.

Preparation of the Gifts
1. We bring a lighted candle. At baptism, we have been called to be a light, showing God's love to everyone.
2. We bring water. At baptism, we have been called to belong to the Christian family and to live in the way of Jesus.
3. We bring the baptism register. At baptism, our names were written down in the baptism book.
4. We bring our lives to God, with the bread and wine.

Second Prayer
God our Father, we bring you our gifts of bread and wine. We bring you our lives, our work, and our love that you may bless them. We make this prayer through Jesus Christ, your Son, who lives and reigns with you in the unity of the Holy Spirit, one God forever and ever. Amen.

Third Prayer
God our Father, may we live in the way of Jesus, and stay close to him always. We make this prayer through Jesus Christ, your Son, who lives and reigns with you in the unity of the Holy Spirit, one God forever and ever. Amen.

Final Blessing
Go in peace to love God and to live in the way of Jesus, in goodness and friendship.

2. Being Great for God

Today we are thinking about being great for God. We know some people who are great—they try to do something really well. The saints were all great people. They were great for God. We can be like them.

First Prayer

God our Father, you are great. You sent us Jesus who is great. Help us to be great—to be your friends and followers. We ask this through Jesus, your Son, who lives and reigns with you in the unity of the Holy Spirit, one God forever and ever. Amen.

First Reading

This reading is part of a poem thanking God for God's greatness in giving us beautiful things.

We thank you, Lord of heaven,
For the joys that greet us,
For all that you have given
To help and delight us
In earth and sky and seas;
The sunlight on the meadows,
The rainbow's fleeting wonder,
The clouds with cooling shadows,
The stars that shine in splendor—
We thank you, Lord, for these.
Jan Struther

Responsorial Psalm Psalm 17:8-9, 12-16
RESPONSE: Lord God, you are great and powerful.
1. God is as strong as an earthquake that shakes the whole world and makes the mountains tremble! R.
2. God is as strong as a volcano that splits the land open, pouring out fire and burning flames and clouds of smoke. R.

---

3. God is as powerful as a thunderstorm at night, when everything is dark, and lightning flashes across the sky, cutting through the heavy rain clouds like an arrow! R.

4. God is as powerful as the mighty sound of thunder rumbling overhead like a deep and angry roar. R.

Second Reading Romans 15:17-19

This reading is about St. Paul. He wrote this about himself:

I'm proud of what I've been able to do to make God's way known throughout the world. But only through Jesus have I been able to do what I have done. There is one thing—and one thing only—I care to talk about: how Jesus has used me to help people of many lands to live in God's way. From Jerusalem to Palestine, all around the world I have made the Good News of Jesus sound like the Good News it is—good news for everybody. For I have had one ambition: to tell the story of Jesus where his name has never been heard.

The Word of the Lord.

Third Reading Romans 15:3-6

This reading comes from St. Paul's letters. It tells us how great Jesus was.

He cared for people—for everybody. He was a very happy man. People who couldn't get on with one another found it possible to be friends in his presence. He never gave up. He was very kind, a really good man, and he could always be relied upon. He was gentle, yet master of himself. What people remembered about him was his graciousness.

The Word of the Lord.

Gospel Acclamation

Alleluia, alleluia,

Believe me, when you helped the least of my brothers, you helped me.

Alleluia.

Gospel Matthew 25:35-37, 40
The reading is from the Gospel of St. Matthew. Jesus often told his friends that they would be truly great if they served others. They would prove they were his friends if he could say to them:

I was hungry and you gave me food;
I was thirsty and you gave me drink;
I was a foreigner and you took me home with you;
I was in rags and you gave me clothes;
I fell ill and you looked after me;
I was in prison and you came to see me.
Believe me—when you helped the least of my brothers,
you helped me.
The Gospel of the Lord.

Prayer of the Faithful
1. Mary was obedient and did what God asked her to do. Help us to be great and to do what we are told. Lord, hear us. R.
2. St. Veronica was kind to Jesus on the way to Calvary. Help us to be great and to be kind and loving. Lord, hear us. R.
3. St. Bernadette loved Mary and prayed to her often. Help us to be great and to love Mary our Mother. Lord, hear us. R.
4. St. Stephen was quick to forgive his enemies. Help us to be great and to forgive like him. Lord, hear us. R.
5. St. Vincent cared for the sick and the poor. Help us to be great, to comfort the sick and help the poor. Lord, hear us. R.
6. St Patrick spent long hours praying. Help us to be great and to pray often. Lord, hear us. R.

Preparation of the Gifts
We bring gifts to show that, like all great artists, we must not give up trying to be great.

1. We bring a football. Footballers keep on trying.
2. We bring a musical instrument. Musicians keep on trying.
3. We bring a pair of dancing shoes. Dancers keep on trying.
4. We bring our lives to God, with the bread and wine.

Second Prayer

God our Father, we bring you ourselves with all our gifts. Help us to bring joy, love and peace to all our friends. We ask this through Jesus, your Son, who lives and reigns with you in the unity of the Holy Spirit, one God forever and ever. Amen.

Third Prayer

God our Father, you have given us your Son. Jesus is great. May he help us to be great, too. We ask this through Jesus, your Son, who lives and reigns with you in the unity of the Holy Spirit, one God forever and ever. Amen.

Final Blessing

Go in peace, to know God and to love God.

3. Love One Another

Today we are thinking about love. The night before Jesus died, he gave all of us a new commandment. It was to love one another. We show our love for Jesus by loving one another.

First Prayer
God our Father, you love us as a father loves his children. Help us to live and love like your Son, Jesus. We make this prayer through Jesus, your Son, who lives and reigns with you in the unity of the Holy Spirit, one God forever and ever. Amen.

First Reading Isaiah 58:3,4,7,8
This reading comes from the book of a wise man called Isaiah. God tells us to look after each other, and to share our things.

God says:
Remember,
it is no good saying your prayers to me,
if you go on hurting each other,
or if you keep on arguing and fighting
and punching each other.
You must share things.
You must feed the hungry,
and get houses for the poor people,
and buy clothes for the people who haven't got enough.
If you do this,
you will make the whole world bright,
you will be like the sun
that fills the sky with light each morning.
The Word of the Lord.

Responsorial Psalm
RESPONSE: God the Father loves us.

1. He loves our voices, he loves our eyes. R.
2. He loves every strand of our hair, he loves our names. R.
3. He loves each one of us, he loves us all the time. R.
4. He loves us when we are awake, he loves us when we are asleep. R.
5. He loves us when we are happy, he loves us when we are sad. R.

Second Reading 1 Thessalonians 5:12-17
This reading comes from one of St. Paul's letters. He tells us how to love and be happy together.

Dear friends,
Help your teachers, and don't make life difficult for them.
Don't fight with each other, don't be lazy,
and help the people who are nervous.
Take care of the children who are not very well.
Be patient.
Don't try to get your own back.
Think of what would be best for everyone.
The Word of the Lord.

Gospel Acclamation
Alleluia, alleluia,
Jesus said:
"I love you all very much.
I want you to be happy like me."
Alleluia.

Gospel John 13:34,35
This reading comes from the Gospel of St. John. Jesus gives his followers a new rule: they must love like him.

One day Jesus said:
Take care of each other.
This is my new rule:

Love each other just as much as I have loved you.
If you do, people will notice,
and they will say, "You are like Jesus."
The Gospel of the Lord.

Prayer of the Faithful

God, our Father, Jesus your Son was a sign of your love for us. Help us to be a sign of this same love in the lives of others.

1. We pray for our mothers and fathers and all our families. Help us to love them. Lord, hear us. R.

2. We pray for our teachers and friends. Help us to love them. Lord, hear us. R.

3. We pray for the sick and the dying of our parish. Help us to love them. Lord, hear us. R.

4. We pray for the friendless and the unhappy people of our parish. Help us to love them. Lord, hear us. R.

5. We pray for the old and the lonely of our parish. Help us to love them. Lord, hear us. R.

6. We pray for those in our parish who are nervous and frightened. Help us to love them. Lord, hear us. R.

Preparation of the Gifts

1. We bring a dish cloth and a gardening fork. We bring love when we help our parents.

2. We bring a blackboard eraser and a box of straws. We bring love when we help our teacher.

3. We bring our love with the bread, the wine, and the water. We bring love when we help our teacher.

4. We bring our lives to God, with the bread and wine.

Second Prayer

God our Father, we bring you our gifts. With them we bring our love for one another. Make it more and more like the love of Jesus for all people. We ask this through your Son, Jesus, who lives and reigns with you, in the unity of the Holy Spirit, one God forever and ever. Amen.

Third Prayer
God our Father, you have given us Jesus in a special way in this Mass. Help us to love each other more, with the love of Jesus, your Son. We ask this through your Son, Jesus, who lives and reigns with you, in the unity of the Holy Spirit, one God forever and ever. Amen.

Final Blessing
Go in peace, to love God and show love at home, in school, and at play. Amen

4. Prayer

Today we are thinking about prayer. Prayer is being with God, listening and talking to God. Jesus often prayed. He went to the Temple, or the mountains, or the garden to be alone with his friends and to have time to speak to his Father.

First Prayer

God our Father, you love us. We praise you and thank you for everything that we are and have. We make this prayer through Jesus, your Son, who lives and reigns with you in the unity of the Holy Spirit, one God forever and ever. Amen.

First Reading Luke 11:46-55

This reading is Mary's prayer, the Magnificat. *Mary, the Mother of Jesus, put her trust in God. She knew she could trust him, so she prayed.*

I praise the Lord, for the Lord is good,
the Lord makes me glad!
I am young and I am poor,
and yet the Lord comes and chooses me!
And from now on,
everyone will say that the Lord has blessed me.
The Lord is strong, the Lord is generous,
reaching out to help the sick,
feeding hungry people with good food,
looking after people everywhere!
Long ago the Lord promised to help us.
Now the Lord has kept that promise perfectly!
The Lord has not forgotten his own people,
but has come to rescue them
and keep them safe!
The Word of the Lord.

Responsorial Psalm Psalm 27:6-7

God is someone we can trust, so we pray to God.

RESPONSE: Blessed be God!

1. Blessed be God!

God listens to me.

God hears me, when I pray for help. R.

2. I trust the Lord,

For the Lord is strong. R.

3. I thank the Lord,

For the Lord takes care of me. R.

Second Reading Romans 8:26, 27

This reading comes from one of the letters of St. Paul. The Holy Spirit will help us to pray if we don't know what to say.

Dear friends,

sometimes we find it hard to say our prayers!

But remember, we have a special friend, the Holy Spirit who will help us.

Sometimes, we don't know what to say to God, but the Holy Spirit will help us to pray without using words, and God will understand.

The Word of the Lord.

Gospel Acclamation

Alleluia, alleluia.

When you say your prayers don't worry so much about the things you want. Remember that you have a Father in heaven who knows all about the things you need.

Alleluia.

Gospel Luke 11:1-4

This reading is from the Gospel of St. Luke. Jesus prays to his Father—so should we!

One day Jesus was saying his prayers and, when he had finished, one of his friends said, "Teach us to pray!" So Jesus told them to say this prayer:

"Father, we want everyone to praise you, and we want your kingdom to grow better and better until it is perfect. Give us enough food each day, forgive us when we do wrong, just as we forgive others when they do wrong to us, and help us when we are put to the test." The Gospel of the Lord.

Prayer of the Faithful

God our Father, we know you care for us. We ask you now to listen to our prayers.

1. O God, you are great. Help us to praise you. Lord, hear us. R.

2. O God, you care for us. Help us to trust you. Lord, hear us. R.

3. O God, you are good. Help us to love you. Lord, hear us. R.

4. O God, you are kind. Help us to be sorry when we fail to love. Lord, hear us. R.

5. O God, you are always giving. Help us to be thankful for all your gifts. Lord, hear us. R.

6. O God, you listen to us. Help us and all our friends in need. Lord, hear us. R.

Preparation of the Gifts

1. We bring our toys. We pray as we play.

2. We bring our books. We pray as we learn.

3. We bring a missalette. We pray in church and at home.

4. We bring our lives to God, with the bread and wine.

Second Prayer

God our Father, we bring you our gifts to thank you for what you have given us. Hear our prayers through Jesus, your Son, who lives and reigns with you in the unity of the Holy Spirit, one God forever and ever. Amen.

Third Prayer

God our Father, you have brought us close to Jesus in holy communion. Help us to pray often and well, like Jesus. Help us to pray in school, at play, and in church. We ask this through Jesus, your Son, who lives and reigns with you in the unity of the Holy Spirit, one God forever and ever. Amen.

Final Blessing

Go in peace, to love God.

5. At a Time of Illness

Today, we come together to remember the sick. There's always someone we know in need of our prayers. We ask God to bless our sick friends, to give them good health again, to comfort and strengthen them, in their pain and suffering.

First Prayer
God our Father, we thank you for our good health. Help us to use our gift of health and strength, in the service of others, and for their good. We make this prayer through Jesus Christ, your Son, who lives and reigns with you in the unity of the Holy Spirit, one God forever and ever. Amen.

First Reading Jeremiah 30: 10. 12. 13. 17.
This reading comes from the book of a wise man called Jeremiah. It tells us that God is our healer and can do anything.

God says:
Do not be afraid, my people, for I will come and help you. I hear that you are very ill! No one can cure you, no one can help you and you cannot find a medicine that will do you any good. But I will make you healthy once more. Yes, I will make you better!
The Word of the Lord.

Responsorial Psalm Psalm 71:12-14, 18-19
God wants the whole world to be full of God's goodness and love.
RESPONSE: Never forget what the Lord has done!
1. God will remember the poor when they cry. God will not leave them. God will take care of the weak and helpless. R.
2. God is loving and kind and will remember them. God will not leave them crushed down by their enemies. R.
3. Blessed be God! God can work wonders. Let the whole world be full of God's goodness and love. R.

Second Reading James 5:14-15
St. James is telling us to trust and to pray, and God will cure the sick.

If one of you is ill, he should send for the elders of the church, and they must anoint him with oil in the name of the Lord and pray over him. The prayers will save the sick one and the Lord will make him well again.
The Word of the Lord.

Gospel Acclamation
Alleluia, alleluia.
Jesus said: "Stand up my friend. Pick up your stretcher and go home!"
Alleluia.

Gospel Mark 2:1-6, 11-12
The reading comes from the Gospel of St. Mark. The sick man believed that Jesus could do anything, could heal him!

When Jesus came back to Capernaum, the news got around that he was back and many people came to listen to him. They filled the house where he was, and there wasn't even a space left in front of the door.

While Jesus was talking, four men came with a man on a stretcher. This man was paralyzed and couldn't walk by himself, and they wanted to bring him to Jesus.

There was no room for them to get in through the door. So they made a hole in the roof just over the place where Jesus was standing, and lowered the stretcher down in front of him. It was obvious they believed that Jesus could help the man.

Jesus could see that clearly, so he said, "Stand up, my friend. Pick up your stretcher and go home." And the man got up, and picked up his stretcher at once, and walked out of the house all by himself! Everyone was astonished when they saw this, and they said: "How

good God is!"
The Gospel of the Lord.

Prayer of the Faithful

God our Father, we pray for all who are sick, children and adults, that they may soon be well again. May they put their trust in you, and keep on believing, that all of us are safe, in your hands.

1. Bless those who are sick, in the hospital and at home. Help them, to be strong and brave. Lord, hear us. R.

2. Bless all who look after the sick at home. Help them to be patient and loving. Lord, hear us. R.

3. Bless the doctors and nurses in the hospitals. Help them to be gentle and kind. Lord, hear us. R.

4. Bless the children who are not well. Help them to know that we care about them, and remember them. Lord, hear us. R.

5. Bless us all, and help us to be good to the sick. Help us to be thoughtful and to comfort them. Lord, hear us. R.

Preparation of the Gifts

1. We bring flowers. Flowers remind us of God's loving care, and that God is with us in health and sickness.

2. We bring a crucifix. Jesus suffered pain, was nailed to the cross, made fun of, and left to die.

3. We bring medicine. This reminds us of God's loving care of us, through those who care for us in sickness.

4. We bring our lives to God, with the bread and wine.

Second Prayer

God our Father, we bring our gifts of bread and wine. With them, we bring our friends who are sick—their suffering, their pain, and their courage. We make this prayer through Jesus Christ, your Son, who lives and reigns with you in the unity of the Holy Spirit, one God forever and ever. Amen.

Third Prayer

God our Father, we ask that Jesus, who has come to us in holy communion, will give us the strength to spread your love and goodness to all we meet today. We make this prayer through Jesus Christ, your Son, who lives and reigns with you in the unity of the Holy Spirit, one God forever and ever. Amen.

Final Blessing

Go in peace, to love and serve the Lord, in sickness and in health.

6. Kindness

This theme is about kindness—being kind, thoughtful and helpful every-where—at home and in school. We ask God to give us a share in God's goodness and kindness.

First Prayer
God our Father, you are good and kind to us. Help us to be kind and thoughtful, too. We make this prayer through Jesus Christ, your Son, who lives and reigns with you in the unity of the Holy Spirit, one God forever and ever. Amen.

First Reading
Poem: I've got these hands

I've got these hands that want to do
All sorts of kind things, just for you.
I've got these feet that want to run
And do kind deeds for everyone.
I've got these ears that want to hear
When people call out "Help me, dear."
I've got these eyes that want to see
when people need kindness from me.

Second Reading Romans 12:4-8
St. Paul tells us that we are all here to be kind and helpful to one another.

Dear friends,
Let us try to remember that we are all part of God's family. Each of us is like a different part of the body. We are here to help one another, as the different parts of the body help one another. If we give, let us be generous givers. If we are helping others, let us be cheerful helpers. The Word of the Lord.

Responsorial Psalm Psalm 43:24-7

This psalm is telling us that we can always ask God to help us, especially when we are upset.

RESPONSE: Lord, come and help us now.

1. Wake up, Lord!
Don't say you're still sleeping!
Can't you see we need you? R.
2. Please don't hide away.
Look, we're all in trouble.
Don't forget us. R.
3. Wake up, Lord, and hear us!
Show us that you love us.
Come and help us now. R.

Gospel Acclamation

Alleluia, alleluia.
One day, Jesus said,
"God is your Father."
Alleluia.

Gospel Matthew 5:45

In this reading, Jesus speaks of God's goodness and kindness to all.

One day, Jesus said:
God is your Father, you must behave like his children. He takes care of everyone—bad people and good people, honest people and dishonest people. He treats them all the same.
The Gospel of the Lord.

Prayer of the Faithful

God our Father, we thank you for your kindness and love. Be with us as we pray for kindness, to help all who need our help.
1. Lord, give us kind hands, to do thoughtful things, for people in need. Lord, hear us. R.

2. Lord, give us kind feet, that will hurry to do kind deeds, to help those who need our help. Lord, hear us. R.

3. Lord, give us kind ears, that will hear, when people call out for help. Lord, hear us. R.

4. Lord, give us kind eyes, that will see, when people look for our kindness. Lord, hear us. R.

5. Lord, give us kind tongues, that will say only good things about others. Lord, hear us. R.

Preparation of the Gifts
1. We bring a loaf of bread. We show kindness to the hungry.
2. We bring a glass of water. We show kindness to the thirsty.
3. We bring our lives to God, with the bread and wine.

Second Prayer
God our Father, we bring you these gifts. Be with us as we try to bring the kindness of Jesus, your Son, to others. We make this prayer through Jesus Christ, your Son, who lives and reigns with you in the unity of the Holy Spirit, one God forever and ever. Amen.

Third Prayer
God our Father, we are together in a special way in this Holy Communion. Help us to live together with kindness and love. We make this prayer through Jesus Christ, your Son, who lives and reigns with you in the unity of the Holy Spirit, one God forever and ever. Amen.

Final Blessing
Go in peace, to love God, and to be kind, thoughtful and helpful to one another.

7. Spreading Peace

We come together today to think about, pray for, and discover ways in which we can spread peace. We all long for it, in our country, in our parish, in our homes, and in ourselves. Let us earnestly ask God to show us what we can do and what is possible.

First Prayer
God our Father, you call us to spread peace and love in the world. Help us to live in peace with you, and with one another. We make this prayer through Jesus Christ, your Son, who lives and reigns with you in the unity of the Holy Spirit, one God forever and ever. Amen.

First Reading
Peace

Peace is calmness, peace is quietness,
Peace is love and gentleness,
Peace is gladness, peace is goodness,
Peace is joy and happiness.

Peace is loving, peace is helping
Peace is showing that you care.
Peace is sharing, peace is giving
Peace is joining hands in prayer.
Caitríona O'Carroll

Responsorial Psalm Psalm 62:7-9
We know we are safe with God our Father.
RESPONSE: Lord God, I am happy to be with you.
1. At night I lie in bed and think of you, Lord God. I lie there in the darkness of the night and remember how good you are, for you have always helped me. R.

2. I am like a little bird that clings to its mother. You are like the mighty eagle who spreads its wings above its young to protect them. R.

3. I am happy to lie here in the dark under the shadow of your wings, Lord God. R.

Second Reading Romans 12:10, 13, 18
The reading is from the Letter of St. Paul to the Romans. Here he tells us how to live in peace together.
Dear friends,
Be a real family, warmhearted in your care for one another, thinking better of others than of yourselves. Take your part in helping other friends of Jesus, when they are in want. Make it your aim to keep the doors of your home open, to those who need it. As far as you can, be friends with everybody. Never try to get revenge. Leave that in God's hands.
The Word of the Lord.

Gospel Acclamation
Alleluia, alleluia.
"I leave you peace,"
said Jesus.
Alleluia.

Gospel John 14:27
This reading comes from the Gospel of St. John. Jesus wants his friends to be gentle with each other and to live in peace.

One day, Jesus said:
I leave you "peace." I give you my own kind of peace. Do not be worried or upset, do not be afraid.
The Gospel of the Lord.

Prayer of the Faithful

God our Father, we thank you today for giving us your peace. We pray for peace for our families, for our friends and for ourselves.

1. Help us to spread peace at home and at school, by loving and caring for everybody. Lord, hear us. R.

2. Help us to spread peace, by forgiving each other, as soon as a quarrel begins. Lord, hear us. R.

3. Help us to spread peace, by making life pleasant for others. Lord, hear us. R.

4. Help us to spread peace, by taking care of those, who are not well. Lord, hear us. R.

5. Help us to spread peace, by sharing people's happiness as well as their sadness. Lord, hear us. R.

Preparation of the Gifts

1. We bring a lighted candle. Jesus came into the world, with a message of peace.

2. We bring an olive branch. The olive branch is the emblem of peace.

3. We bring our lives to God, with the bread and wine.

Second Prayer

God our Father, bless these gifts which we bring to you. Take us, too, and make us peacemakers in our world today. We make this prayer through Jesus Christ, your Son, who lives and reigns with you in the unity of the Holy Spirit, one God forever and ever. Amen.

Communion Litany

RESPONSE: Thank you, God.

1. For calmness, quietness, and gentleness. R.

2. For goodness, joy, and happiness. R.

3. For caring, sharing, and giving. R.

4. For kindness, forgiveness, and love. R.

5. For happiness and contentment, with ourselves and with others. R.

6. For times of quiet and for hands joined in prayer. R.

7. For truth, honesty, and justice. R.

8. For Christ, lover and giver of peace. R.

Third Prayer

God our Father, may the coming of Jesus to us, in holy communion, give us peace. May he stay with us, as we try to spread peace and love in our world today. We make this prayer through Jesus Christ, your Son, who lives and reigns with you in the unity of the Holy Spirit, one God forever and ever. Amen.

Final Blessing

Go in peace, to love God, and to be peacemakers in school, in the playground, and at home.

8. Helping Children in Need

Today's Mass readings and prayers are for children in need. We try to help by our prayers and by being generous enough to share what we have.

First Prayer
God our Father, you have given us many good gifts. Help us to show concern for children in need; help us to do all we can and to share our good things with them. We ask this through Jesus, your Son, who lives and reigns with you in the unity of the Holy Spirit, one God forever and ever. Amen.

First Reading Isaiah 58:3, 4, 7, 8
This reading comes from the book of a wise man called Isaiah. He tells us that God wants us to help the poor and the hungry, so that the world can be full of his goodness and love.

God says:
Remember,
You must share things.
You must feed the hungry, and get houses for the poor people, and buy clothes for the people who haven't got enough.
If you do this,
You will make the whole world bright.
You will be like the sun that fills the sky with light each morning.
The Word of the Lord.

Responsorial Psalm Psalm 71:12-14, 18-19
God our Father wants us to know that the poor are not forgotten. God will take care of those who cannot help themselves.
RESPONSE: Never forget what the Lord has done.
1. God will remember the poor when they cry.
God will never forget them.
God will take care of the weak and the helpless. R.

---

2. God is loving and kind.

God will remember them.

God will not forget them when they are in danger. R.

3. God will not leave them to die of starvation, for God loves them too much. R.

4. Blessed be God!

God can work wonders.

Let the whole world be full of God's goodness and love! R.

Second Reading Romans 8:16-20

In this reading St. Paul tells us that God wants us to work with God and to help each other.

The world is a place where God works for all that is worthwhile, alongside those who love God. We are workers for God. This is what God is calling us to be. The earth itself is being spoiled by the way people live. It is waiting for the time when the people who live on it will live, not as they do now, but as members of God's family, with mercy and gentleness, sharing it together.

The Word of the Lord.

Gospel Acclamation

Alleluia, alleluia,

"Go help everyone, everywhere, to follow me," says the Lord.

Alleluia.

Gospel John 21:15-17

This reading is from the Gospel of St. John. It tells us that Jesus wants us to look after his friends.

After breakfast, Jesus turned to Peter as they walked along, and called him by his own name, Simon. "Simon," he said, "do you love me more than anything else?" "Yes, sir," said Peter, "you know I love you." "Look after my friends," said Jesus. Jesus spoke to Peter a second time. "Simon," he said, "do you love me?" "Yes, sir," said Peter, "you know I love you." "Look after my friends," said Jesus. Then a third time, Jesus spoke to Peter. "Simon," he said, "do you love me?" For Jesus to ask him this question three times upset Peter. "Sir," he said, "you know all about me. You, of all people, know I love you." "Look after my friends," said Jesus.

The Gospel of the Lord.

Prayer of the Faithful

God our Father, we come to you today with our own needs and the needs of children everywhere.

1. We pray for children who are hungry. Give them the food and drink they need today. Lord, hear us. R.

2. We pray for children who are cold. Give them clothes and warmth today. Lord, hear us. R.

3. We pray for children who are sick. Give them comfort and healing today. Lord, hear us. R.

4. We pray for children who are frightened. Give them love and peace today. Lord, hear us. R.

5. We pray for children who are lonely. Give them happiness and friendship today. Lord, hear us. R.

6. We pray for people everywhere, at home and all over the world, who work with children, and who lovingly care for them. Give them the help and strength they need. Lord, hear us. R.

Preparation of the Gifts

1. We bring our mission boxes. Our savings help to feed the hungry.

2. We bring a loaf of bread. We do without things we like, so that we can give to others.

3. We bring our lives to God, with the bread and wine.

Second Prayer

God our Father, we bring ourselves to you with our gifts of bread and wine. May we grow in your love by our sharing, and by helping children in need. We ask this through Jesus, your Son, who lives and reigns with you in the unity of the Holy Spirit, one God forever and ever. Amen.

Third Prayer
God our Father, may this holy communion help us to love each other more, and to work for the love and happiness of children everywhere. We ask this through Jesus, your Son, who lives and reigns with you in the unity of the Holy Spirit, one God forever and ever. Amen.

Final Blessing
Go in peace, to love God and to help children in need.

9. Saying Thank You

We have a lot to thank God for. We say thanks for our parents, our homes, our gifts and talents, our food, our school and friends, our playtimes and games, and our world.

First Prayer
God our Father, we thank you for all you have given us—a lovely world, a happy home, and good friends. Make us always thankful for your gifts. We make this prayer through Jesus Christ, your Son, who lives and reigns with you in the unity of the Holy Spirit, one God forever and ever. Amen.

First Reading
Poem: Thank You.

"What do you say?"…
I think they're Mommy's favorite words—
"what do you say?"…
…When I've been given candy,
or ice cream,
or a toy,
…or when my coat's been buttoned,
or my shoes,
or my hair.
"Now, what do you say?"
…When I've been out to tea,
or the park,
or the sea.
Well, what do I say?
Thank you!

Second Reading Colossians 3:16-17
St. Paul is reminding us of all God has done for us and how thankful we should be.

Dear friends,

How full of songs your hearts will be, songs of joy and praise and love, songs to God. In this spirit, you can take everything in your stride, matching word and deed, as the friends of the Lord Jesus. Make him the center of your life and, with his help, let your hearts be filled with thankfulness to God your Father.

The Word of the Lord.

Responsorial Psalm Psalm 135:1-9

In this psalm, we say thanks to God who gives us so much.

RESPONSE: Thank you, God, you are good to us.

1. You made the sky for us, for you are wise. You made the earth for us, for you are kind. R.

2. You gave the sun to us to shine all day long. You gave the moon to us, to shine through the night. R.

Gospel Acclamation

Alleluia, alleluia.

"Stand up my friend," said Jesus,

"God loves you for what you have done."

Alleluia.

Gospel Luke 17:11-19

This is the story of the one who thanked Jesus for what he did for him.

One day, Jesus went up to Jerusalem and, while he was on his way, he went into a little town nearby. Ten lepers came out to him there, and they waved across to him, saying,

"Please help us, Jesus!"

When he saw them Jesus said,

"Go and see the priest!"

So they did and, as they were on their way, they were healed!

One of them came right back to Jesus and he praised God at the top of his voice, throwing himself down in front of Jesus.

"Thank you, Jesus," he said, "Thank you very much!"
Jesus then said,
"Didn't all the others get better as well? Or have they just not bothered to come and say thank you? I wonder why you are the only one who came back. Stand, up my friend," he said. "God loves you for what you have done."
The Gospel of the Lord.

Prayer of the Faithful

God our Father, we thank you for what you have done for us. We thank you for our friends. We ask you to bless them and all those who are good to us.
1. Bless our parents—mothers and fathers—who love us and care for us. Lord, hear us. R.
2. Bless our brothers and sisters, and all our families who are kind and forgiving when we hurt them. Lord, hear us. R.
3. Bless our priests and teachers who work with us, and do so much for our happiness. Lord, hear us. R.
4. Bless our friends who make us happy, and help us to enjoy ourselves. Lord, hear us. R.
5. Bless all the people who work for us, and those who try to make things easy and pleasant. Lord, hear us. R.

Preparation of the Gifts

1. We bring a Bible. We thank God for the gift of parents and our homes.
2. We bring a loaf of bread. We thank God for the gift of food.
3. We bring our lives to God, with the bread and wine. We thank God for the gifts of life and love.

Second Prayer

God our Father, we give you our gifts of bread and wine. We pray that they will become our special food. We make this prayer through

Jesus Christ, your Son, who lives and reigns with you in the unity of the Holy Spirit, one God forever and ever. Amen.

Third Prayer

God our Father, Jesus is with us now, in a special way. We thank him for his love and goodness. We make this prayer through Jesus Christ, your Son, who lives and reigns with you in the unity of the Holy Spirit, one God forever and ever. Amen.

Final Blessing

Go in peace, to love God, and thank God for all God's gifts and goodness.

10. Thanks for People Who Help Us

The theme of this Mass is thanking God for the people without whom our lives would be different, difficult, or even impossible. We thank God for all who work for our well-being and comfort.

First Prayer
God our Father, you have given us many people to help us. Make us always grateful for their help, and for the things they do to make us happy. We make this prayer through Jesus Christ, your Son, who lives and reigns with you in the unity of the Holy Spirit, one God forever and ever. Amen.

First Reading
This is a poem of thanks for the people who work to help us live, and enjoy living.

Helpers
Mothers are always there to help,
And fathers are big and strong,
And Grandmas and Grandpas listen and love,
Especially when things go wrong.
Up in the town the people work,
And out on the deep blue sea,
And busy on farms all over the land
People are helping me.
Some work in the sky, some travel,
And some are deep underground.
You'd never believe when I counted,
The number of helpers I found.
Each of them serves me every day,
And I want them all to know
I'd like to say "Thank you," if only I could,
For working to help me so.

Responsorial Psalm Psalm 45:3-6, 9-11

We thank God who is always with us, helping us, and is gentle and kind always.

RESPONSE: You are our God.

1. We don't mind even if the earth shakes, even if the sea is raging. Even if the hills fall down, we don't mind. R.

2. God is like the gentle river that flows beside the house of prayer bringing water to our city to make us strong and make us glad. R.

3. God lives with us in our city. Whatever happens, we are safe. R.

Second Reading Philippians 4:10-13

St. Paul tells us about the help he gets from Jesus. He can face anything because of the strength that comes to him from Jesus.

Dear friends,

With such a story to tell, I've learned how to stand on my own feet, wherever I am. I know how to do without things. I know how to live when I've got more than I need. It doesn't matter now what happens—I can face plenty and poverty. I can enjoy wealth and want. I've learned God's secret. There isn't anything I can't face; but I know where my strength comes from—it comes from Jesus.

The Word of the Lord.

Gospel Acclamation

Alleluia, alleluia.

Jesus said, "Get up, little girl."

And she did, and walked around the room.

Alleluia.

Gospel Mark 5:22-24, 35-43

In this story, Jesus heals a little girl because her father asks Jesus to come and help.

One day, a man called Jairus came to Jesus and threw himself down in front of him. "My little girl is dying," he said. "Come and hold her

in your arms and she will get better again." So Jesus went along with him. Then someone came and said, "It's no use bothering Jesus any more. Your little girl has just died." But Jesus took no notice, and said to Jairus, "Don't worry. All you have to do is trust me." When they got to Jairus' house, there were lots of people there, and they were all crying. So Jesus said, "What's all this for? The little girl isn't dead, she's only asleep." But no one believed him. So Jesus sent everyone out of the house. Then he went into the room where the little girl was lying, and he took with him only her mother and father, and Peter, James, and John. Then he held the girl's hand, and said "Get up, little girl." And she did, and walked around the room! Her father and mother were so surprised they just didn't know what to do, so Jesus told them to give the girl something to eat.
The Gospel of the Lord.

Prayer of the Faithful
God our Father, we thank you for people who help us. We ask you to bless them, and to give them the strength they need each day, as they work for our good and happiness.
1. Bless our mothers and fathers, for all they do to make our homes comfortable for us. Lord, hear us. R.
2. Bless our teachers, for all they do for us in school, as we learn and play together. Lord, hear us. R.
3. Bless our priests, who lead us to you, by word and deed, and are always ready to help. Lord, hear us. R.
4. Bless the people who work for us in the country, in field and farm, producing good fresh food. Lord, hear us. R.
5. Bless the people who work for us in the town, in the streets, shops, and offices, serving us quietly and usefully. Lord, hear us. R.
6. Bless the people who care for us when we are ill, and who help us to recover, and feel better. Lord, hear us. R.

Preparation of the Gifts
1. We bring a loaf of bread and a pair of shoes. Our parents are lov-

ing and caring, always thinking about our comfort and well-being.
2. We bring flowers. We show our parents that we are grateful for what they do for us.
3. We bring our lives to God, with the bread and wine.

Second Prayer

God our Father, with outstretched hands we give gifts of bread and wine. May we be ready to show our love for you, and always help others with outstretched hands. We ask this through Jesus, your Son, who lives and reigns with you in the unity of the Holy Spirit, one God forever and ever. Amen.

Litany of Thanks

RESPONSE: We thank you, God our Father.
1. For mailmen, who deliver our letters and packages. R.
2. For policemen who direct the traffic, and help us cross the street safely. R.
3. For nurses and doctors, who look after us in the hospital. R.
4. For builders, carpenters, and plumbers who build new houses for us. R.
5. For salespeople in our shops, who help us to choose and buy new clothes and shoes. R.
6. For garage mechanics, who help to keep cars in good repair. R.
7. For firemen, who put out fires and rescue people in danger. R.
8. For drivers of buses and trains, who help us to travel in comfort and safety. R.
9. For cleaners, who clean and polish our schools and make them beautiful. R.
10. For those who collect our garbage, and dispose of it neatly. R.

Third Prayer

God our Father, you show us how much you love by giving us Jesus. We go out to help wherever we can, so that all will know and feel your love. We make this prayer through Jesus, your Son, who lives and reigns with you in the unity of the Holy Spirit, one God forever and ever. Amen.

Final Blessing
Go in peace, to love God, and to help everyone as much as you can.

11. Sharing

This theme is sharing. We learn to share at home, when we see our parents share their lives and love, to make us happy. We learn to share our own things with others, because this is what God wants us to do.

First Prayer
God our Father, we thank you for what you have given us. Help us to share, what we have with others. We make this prayer through Jesus Christ, your Son, who lives and reigns with you in the unity of the Holy Spirit, one God forever and ever. Amen.

First Reading Isaiah 58:3, 4, 7, 8
This reading comes from the book of a wise man called Isaiah. God tells us it is very important for us to share.

God says:
Remember,
it is no good saying your prayers to me,
if you go on hurting each other,
or if you keep on arguing and fighting,
and punching each other.
You must share things.
You must feed the hungry,
and get houses for the poor people,
and buy clothes for the people who haven't got enough.
If you do this,
You will make the whole world bright,
You will be like the sun
that fills the sky with light each morning.
The Word of the Lord.

Responsorial Psalm Psalm 71:12-14
This psalm is from the Book of Praise. God takes care of the weak and the

helpless and loves them.
RESPONSE: God is kind and loving.
1. God will remember the poor when they cry. God will never forget them. God will take care of the weak and helpless. R.
2. God is kind and loving. God will not forget the helpless when they are in danger. R.
3. God will not leave them to die of starvation, for God loves them too much. R.

Second Reading Acts 2:44-47
The reading tells us how the friends of Jesus lived and shared everything together.

The friends of Jesus made a great stir in the city. They lived together like members of one family. They shared everything with one another. They sold their property and possessions and shared the money out so that nobody went without anything he needed. They shared their meals together with real happiness. They were a happy company. Nobody went without what he needed.
The Word of the Lord.

Gospel Acclamation
Alleluia, alleluia.
God said:
"You must share things
You must feed the hungry."
Alleluia.

Gospel Luke 3:10-11
The reading is from the Gospel of St. Luke. John's message to the people was for them to share with each other.

Lots of people came to John the Baptist and said:
"What have we got to do?"

John said:
"Share things with each other, and don't be greedy, either!"
The Gospel of the Lord.

Prayer of the Faithful

God our Father, we come to say thanks for your goodness. Help us to be generous and to share our gifts with others.

1. Help us to be generous with our time, and to help others, especially when we are in a hurry. Lord, hear us. R.

2. Help us to be generous with our belongings, and to share things like our books, our erasers, and our pencils. Lord, hear us. R.

3. Help us to be generous with our toys, and our treats, and to share them with our friends. Lord, hear us. R.

4. Help us to be generous with our knowledge, and to share with others how to do things we already know. Lord, hear us. R.

5. Help us to be generous with our talents, and to use them to make others happy. Lord, hear us. R.

Preparation of the Gifts

1. We bring a clock. We share our time, when others need our help.

2. We bring toys. We share games, and the enjoyable things we have, with others.

3. We bring a musical instrument. We share our talents, to make others happy.

4. We bring our lives to God, with the bread and wine.

Second Prayer

God our Father, with these gifts of bread and wine we ask you to accept our lives—all our time, our talents, and our love. We make this prayer through Jesus Christ, your Son, who lives and reigns with you in the unity of the Holy Spirit, one God forever and ever. Amen.

Third Prayer

God our Father, Jesus your Son is with us in holy communion. May we be generous like Jesus, with our time, our belongings, our talents, and our love. We make this prayer through Jesus Christ, your Son, who lives and reigns with you in the unity of the Holy Spirit, one God forever and ever. Amen.

Final Blessing
Go in peace, to live like Jesus, and to share with each other.

12. Trust

The theme is trust. God has said so many times that God will be with us always. We just have to trust and believe God. This should help us in all our ups and downs.

First Prayer
God our Father, you have told us that you will be our friend, and that you will be with us always. Help us to believe this with all our hearts, and to put our trust in you. We make this prayer through Jesus Christ, your Son, who lives and reigns with you in the unity of the Holy Spirit, one God forever and ever. Amen.

First Reading Genesis 12:17-18
The reading comes from the Book of Beginnings. Abraham trusted because he knew God would not let him down.

One night, Abraham was standing outside his tent, looking up at the stars, and he wondered how many stars there were. He couldn't even begin to count them all! Then God told him, "You will have as many children as there are stars!"

And Abraham believed what God said. Then he fell asleep, and dreamed that God came to him, like a great fire that burned in the dark! And God said, "I promise you, I will be your friend."
The Word of the Lord.

Responsorial Psalm Psalm 19: 8-9
This is a song of trust in God. We can trust God even when everything else lets us down.
RESPONSE: We trust in God.
1. The soldiers are proud of their glittering chariots and the speed of their horses. R.
2. But even their horses can stumble and fall and when they fall down they're no use at all! R.

3. We don't trust in horses. We trust in God. God will take care of us. R.

4. God will take care of us better than horses for, when we fall down, God will help us stand up and stand firm. R.

Second Reading Romans 12:8, 10, 13, 11, 12
The reading comes from one of the letters of St. Paul. One thing he is telling us is to trust God who will make us happy.

Dear friends,
Don't just pretend to be good, really try to be kind and try not to be bad.

You are part of God's family and you must take care of each other like good brothers and sisters. Don't forget to share your things with each other and, when you have to work, don't be lazy! Do it for the sake of Jesus. Trust God and he will make you happy. Don't give up if things are difficult. And, of course, always remember to say your prayers.
The Word of the Lord.

Gospel Acclamation
Alleluia, alleluia.
One day Jesus said:
"Don't worry about yourself. God will take good care of you."
Alleluia.

Gospel Luke 12:6-7
The reading comes from the Gospel of St. Luke. God looks after little sparrows who are not very important. God will take care of us too, just as God has said.

One day, Jesus said:
God does not forget even the little sparrows. They are not very important and they didn't cost much, but God remembers each one of them. So don't worry about yourself. God will take good care of you,

for you are worth more than all the sparrows in the world.
The Gospel of the Lord.

Prayer of the Faithful

God our Father, we come before you in faith and trust, to pray for our own needs, and the needs of others. We are confident that you will listen to our prayers. We are happy, and have nothing to fear.

1. Father, we trust you, as we pray for our bishop and the priests of our parish. Lord, hear us. R.

2. Father, we trust you, as we pray for our mothers and fathers, our brothers and sisters. Lord, hear us. R.

3. Father, we trust you, as we pray for all our relatives and friends. Lord, hear us. R.

4. Father, we trust you, as we pray for those who are sick, at home and in the hospital. Lord, hear us. R.

5. Father, we trust you, as we pray for those who do not believe your Word, and what you have said. Lord, hear us. R.

Preparation of the Gifts

1. We bring a Bible. We believe in your Word—and in your promise to be with us.

2. We bring an anchor. We believe in your presence with us, and that we can do all things in you.

3. We bring our lives to God, with the bread and wine.

Second Prayer

God our Father, take our gifts of bread and wine. Take us, too, as we trust your Word, and your promise to be our friend. We make this prayer through Jesus Christ, your Son, who lives and reigns with you in the unity of the Holy Spirit, one God forever and ever. Amen.

Communion Litany

RESPONSE: Thank you God, our Father.

1. For Abraham, who believed what you told him and trusted. R.
2. For Moses, hungry in the desert wilderness, who trusted. R.
3. For Mary, who said "Yes" to God, and trusted. R.
4. For the shepherds on the hillside near Bethlehem, who trusted and quickly found the stable. R.
5. For the three wise men, who followed the star and trusted. R.
6. For the blind beggar, who shouted for help to Jesus, and trusted. R.
7. For Jairus, father of the little dead girl, who asked Jesus to come and hold her in his arms, and trusted. R.
8. For Martha and Mary, sisters of the dead Lazarus, and friends of Jesus, who waited and trusted. R.

Third Prayer
God our Father, we have come together in this holy communion. Stay with us as we grow in your love, your friendship, and in our trust in you. We make this prayer through Jesus Christ, your Son, who lives and reigns with you in the unity of the Holy Spirit, one God forever and ever. Amen.

Final Blessing
Go in peace, to love God, to believe and to trust.

13. Listening

Today we are thinking about the importance of being good listeners. We talk a lot and spend very little time listening. We must try to talk less and listen more.

First Prayer

God our Father, thank you for the gift of hearing. Help us to listen to one another. Above all, help us to listen to your Son, Jesus, so that we may know your plan for us. We ask this through Jesus, your Son, who lives and reigns with you in the unity of the Holy Spirit, one God forever and ever. Amen.

First Reading   1 Samuel 3:2-9,19

This reading is from the story of the kings. It is the story of Samuel, the boy who listened to the voice of God.

A long, long time ago there was a priest called Eli. He was very old and was going blind. But a young boy called Samuel looked after him.

One night, while Samuel was in bed, he heard someone calling his name. "Samuel! Samuel!" So he got up and went to Eli and said, "Here I am. What do you want?" But Eli said, "I didn't call you! Go back to bed." But it happened once more, and Samuel went back to Eli, and again Eli told him to go back to bed. But when it happened a third time, Eli said, "Next time you must say, 'Yes, Lord, I am listening.'"

And it did happen again, for God came and stood beside Samuel and called his name, and Samuel said, "Yes, Lord, I'm listening." And then God spoke to Samuel and told him what God was going to do.

After that, God was always very close to Samuel and, when the boy grew up, he always listened to what God told him.
The Word of the Lord.

Responsorial Psalm Psalm 28:3-5, 8-10
RESPONSE: Glory be to God.
1. Listen to the sound of water,
of waves crashing on the rocks.
Listen to the sound of thunder
far away, out at sea...
and you will hear the voice of God. R.
2. Listen to the sound of trees
groaning, creaking in the storm.
Listen to them crack and break ...
and you will hear the voice of God. R.
3. Listen to the hissing desert winds
that sweep the sand along the valley,
making all the land begin to tremble...
and you will hear the voice of God. R.
4. Glory be to God!
the people cry,
many voices joined together,
singing in the house of prayer,
praising God, their Lord and King. R.

Second Reading Mark 4:23-24
This reading comes from the Gospel of St. Mark. It is a short reading, telling us to use our ears well, to listen.

If you've got ears, use them. When you listen, you must really listen. The Word of the Lord.

Gospel Acclamation
Alleluia, alleluia.
Speak, Lord, I'm listening.
Alleluia.

Gospel Luke 24:13-33
This reading comes from the Gospel of St. Luke. It tells how two of Jesus'

friends met him on the way to a little town near Jerusalem, and listened to him.

On Easter Sunday morning, two of the followers of Jesus had to go to a place called Emmaus and, as they walked along, they talked about Jesus, about what he had said, and how he had died. While they were talking, Jesus himself came and joined them, only they didn't see that it was Jesus.

The stranger asked them both what they were talking about, and they replied, "Don't you know about Jesus? We all thought he was going to be our king, but then he was killed three days ago. Now even his body has disappeared. Two of the women we know went to his grave and they told us it had disappeared! They said that Jesus was alive again!"

Then Jesus said, "You just don't seem to understand! Can't you see that he had to suffer and die like that? It was the only way he could win!" And he began to explain how the Bible had said that all these things would happen.

When they came to Emmaus, the two friends asked the stranger to stay for a meal, for it was getting dark.

So Jesus went in with them and, when they sat down at the table, he took the bread, he blessed it, broke it into pieces, and gave it to them to eat. And all of a sudden they saw that it was Jesus himself.
The Gospel of the Lord.

Prayer of the Faithful
God our Father, thank you for the gift of hearing. You speak to us in a secret kind of way. Help us to hear you.
1. Help us to listen when you speak to us in all sorts of ways. Lord, hear us. R.
2. Help us to listen when you speak to us in your holy word. Lord, hear us. R.
3. Help us to listen when you speak to us through the beautiful world around us. Lord, hear us. R.

4. Help us to listen when you speak to us through our friends, our teachers, and our parents. Lord, hear us. R.

5. Help us to listen when you speak to us through all the things that happen to us. Lord, hear us. R.

Preparation of the Gifts

1. We bring a Bible. We listen to God's word.
2. We bring a radio. We listen to the news.
3. We bring a tambourine. We listen to happy sounds.
4. We bring our lives to God, with the bread and wine.

Second Prayer

God our Father, here are our gifts of bread and wine. With them, we bring all the sounds we hear, music, laughter, and the sounds of the sea and the wind. Please accept them in the name of Jesus, your Son, who lives and reigns with you in the unity of the Holy Spirit, one God forever and ever. Amen.

Communion Litany

RESPONSE: Lord God, we praise and thank you.

1. For the sound of our mothers' and fathers' voices, Lord God, we praise and thank you. R.

2. For the sound of music, Lord God, we praise and thank you. R.

3. For the sweet singing of birds, Lord God, we praise and thank you. R.

4. For the sound of wind and rain, Lord God, we praise and thank you. R.

5. For the sound of the mighty sea, Lord God, we praise and thank you. R.

6. For the sound of rushing water, Lord God, we praise and thank you. R.

7. For the happy sound of children's voices, Lord God, we praise and thank you. R.

Third Prayer

God our Father, your Son Jesus is with us now. Help us to be good listeners, so that we may hear what he tells us, and do what he says. We ask this through Jesus, your Son, who lives and reigns with you in the unity of the Holy Spirit, one God forever and ever. Amen.

Final Blessing

Go in peace, to love God.

14. Sorrow for Wrongdoing

We know that God is always loving and forgiving. God continues to bind up our wounds and to heal. When we stray, God wants us back. We reflect on John the Baptist's message, as he urges us to come back and to be sorry.

First Prayer
God our Father, you called John the Baptist to tell the people to turn away from evil, and to do what is good and right. Help us to listen to your word, and to live in the way of Jesus. We make this prayer through Jesus Christ, your Son, who lives and reigns with you in the unity of the Holy Spirit, one God forever and ever. Amen.

First Reading Isaiah 40:3-5
The reading comes from the book of a wise man called Isaiah. Isaiah is telling us to get ready for God, and live in God's way.

A long, long time ago, Isaiah said,
Can you hear the voice of God?
Listen to what he is saying.
"Make a straight road for him to walk along.
Fill in the valleys, and flatten the hills."
Then you will see God.
Everyone will see him, for God has said so himself.
The Word of the Lord.

Responsorial Psalm Psalm 129
People who do wrong can feel cold and miserable. But God wants them to know they can trust God—God will come and help them.
RESPONSE: Forgive me, Lord, I have done wrong.
1. I am watching in the dead of night waiting in the darkness, waiting for the Lord to come. R.
2. I long for you to come to me to take away the darkness of my sins, for you are loving and forgiving. R.

---

3. You are like the brightness of the sun, that comes to light up all the world each morning. R.

4. Like the watchman, I am sure that you will come, and you will listen to my prayer. R.

Second Reading Romans 7:15, 24-25
The reading is from St. Paul's Letter to the Romans. He tells us that Jesus is the one who showed him God's way and helped him to live in it.

Dear friends,
I was a real puzzle to myself:
I didn't do what, in my heart, I really wanted to do, and I hated myself for doing what I did. All this made me unhappy. I didn't know who could help me. And then, thank God, I found the secret of being really myself. It was Jesus who showed me God's way and helped me to live in it.
The Word of the Lord.

Gospel Acclamation
Alleluia, alleluia.
"Stop doing wrong,
God is going to send you a King."
Alleluia.

Gospel Matthew 3:5, 4, 2, 6
The reading comes from St. Matthew's gospel. John the Baptist told the people to get ready for God.

John the Baptist lived down by the river Jordan. He didn't wear expensive clothes, and he didn't eat very much, but lots of people came to see him. He used to say, "Stop doing wrong. God is going to send you a King."

Then everyone would tell God they were sorry for doing wrong, and John would pour water over them in the river, and make them clean.

The Gospel of the Lord.

Prayer of the Faithful

God our Father, we know you are always near, and that you never stop loving us, even when we turn away from you and do wrong. We want to live in the way of Jesus, and we ask your help, as we pray.

1. Help us to live in the way of Jesus, and to love, trust, and go to you at all times. Lord, hear us. R.

2. Help us to treat others well, and to be ready to share with them, whenever we can. Lord, hear us. R.

3. Help us to tell the truth, and to be honest in all that we do and say. R.

4. Help us to live in the way of Jesus, and to be helpful and obliging, at home and at school. Lord, hear us. R.

5. Help us to be thoughtful and kind, and to forgive when others hurt and do wrong. Lord, hear us. R.

Preparation of the Gifts

1. We bring a lighted candle. Jesus shows us God's way and helps us to live in it.

2. We bring a Bible. The Bible is the Word of God, and what it tells us to do is good and right.

3. We bring our lives to God, with the bread and wine.

Second Prayer

God our Father, we bring you our gifts of bread and wine, as a sign that we want to belong to you, and to live in the way of Jesus. We make this prayer through Jesus Christ, your Son, who lives and reigns with you in the unity of the Holy Spirit, one God forever and ever. Amen.

Third Prayer

God our Father, may the coming of Jesus help us today, as we try to do what is good and right, and to bring love, forgiveness, and peace to others. We make this prayer through Jesus Christ, your Son, who lives and reigns with you in the unity of the Holy Spirit, one God forever and ever. Amen.

Final Blessing
Go in peace, to live in the way of Jesus in love and forgiveness.

15. Forgiveness

We remember that God our Father loves us and forgives us. We remember, too, that we, the children of God, grow more like Jesus by the way we love and forgive one another.

First Prayer
God our Father, you are always kind and ready to forgive. Help us to forgive one another. We ask this through Jesus, your Son, who lives and reigns with you, in the unity of the Holy Spirit, one God forever and ever.

First Reading Sirach 28:3-5
This reading comes from the Book of Sirach, and tells us that if we forgive others, God will forgive us when we do wrong.

If a man is angry with someone else,
how can he expect God to be gentle with him?
If a man is unkind to a person like himself,
how can he dare to ask God to be kind to him?
If a man will not forgive others, how can he expect anyone to forgive him?
The Word of the Lord.

Responsorial Psalm Psalm 14:2-3
If we want to follow God our Father, we must listen to God.
RESPONSE: We will follow God.
1. We will not do wrong. We will do what is right. R.
2. We will tell the truth. We will not tell lies. R.
3. We will be good to our brother and sister. We will not hurt our neighbor. R.

Second Reading Colossians 3:12-13
This reading comes from one of the letters of St. Paul. God our Father has

forgiven us. We should try to forgive other people when they do wrong to us.

Dear friends,
God loves you,
so you must be kind to each other.
Be patient
and put up with each other.
Be ready to forgive,
as soon as an argument begins,
because God has forgiven you.
The Word of the Lord.

Gospel Acclamation
Alleluia, alleluia,
Come back to me and be sorry.
Turn back to me, for I am gentle.
I am slow to lose my temper
and very quick to forgive you.
Alleluia.

Gospel Luke 17:3-4
This reading comes from the gospel of St. Luke. We must always be ready to forgive people even if they hurt us.

One day, Jesus said:
If your friend does you wrong,
you can tell him off, if you like,
but if he says he is sorry,
you must forgive him.
Even if he does wrong and upsets you
seven times each day,
but then comes to you
and says he is really sorry,
you must keep on forgiving him.

The Gospel of the Lord.

Prayer of the Faithful

God our Father, we come before you with all our needs, and we ask you to help us to love and forgive.

1. Help us to forgive when we are wrongly blamed or left out. Lord, hear us. R.

2. Help those who find it hard to forgive. Lord, hear us. R.

3. Help our families to be loving and forgiving in our homes. Lord, hear us. R.

4. Help the sick, the sad, and those who feel forgotten. Lord, hear us. R.

5. We pray that the dead may be at peace. Lord, hear us. R.

Preparation of the Gifts

1. We bring a candle. Jesus shows us how to forgive.

2. We bring a crucifix. Jesus loves and forgives us.

3. We bring our hands. We will love and forgive.

4. We bring our lives to God, with the bread and wine.

Second Prayer

God our Father, we ask you to take all our gifts. Help us to give your love and forgiveness to each other. We ask this through Jesus, your Son, who lives and reigns with you in the unity of the Holy Spirit, one God forever and ever. Amen.

Third Prayer

God our Father, through this communion you have brought us closer together. Help us to be kind and forgiving toward each other, like Jesus, who forgave even his enemies. We ask this through Jesus, your Son, who lives and reigns with you in the unity of the Holy Spirit, one God forever and ever. Amen.

Final Blessing

Go in peace, to love God.

16. The Missions

Today we pray for the missions. We think especially of people who leave their families, their homes, and their country to bring the good news of God's love to people and children around the world who do not know about God.

First Prayer
God our Father, you love all children. Help us to love you, and to help our brothers and sisters around the world to know and love you. We make our prayer through Jesus, your Son, who lives and reigns with you in the unity of the Holy Spirit, one God forever and ever. Amen.

First Reading Isaiah 60:2a, 1, 2b
Isaiah, the wise man, tells us that the sun rises in the sky every day and fills the world with light. Jesus is like that as well—only he fills the world with happiness and goodness.

In the beginning, the world was filled with darkness and it was as black as night. But God came and changed all that! God filled the world with God's light instead, just like the sun that shines in the sky every morning.
The Word of the Lord.

Responsorial Psalm Psalm 27:6, 7
This is a song of praise and trust in God.
RESPONSE: Blessed be God.
1. God listens to me, God hears me when I pray for help. R.
2. I trust the Lord for the Lord is strong. R.
3. I thank the Lord for the Lord takes care of me. R.

Second Reading 1 John 3: 1, 4, 7-8
St. John tells us that God is our Father and that we are God's children. God takes care of us and loves us all.
Dear friends,
See how much God thinks of us. God calls us his children, and we

really are, you know.

God takes care of us, so we must take care of each other.

God loves us, so we must love each other.

If we don't know that, we don't know anything about God our Father, because "God is Love."

The Word of the Lord.

Gospel Acclamation

Alleluia, alleluia.

Go out to the whole world, tell everyone what I have done.

Alleluia.

Gospel Mark 16:15-16, 20

In this reading Jesus is telling his friends to spread the good news everyvhere in the whole world.

One day, Jesus said to his friends:

"Go out to the whole world. Tell everyone what I have done and baptize everyone who believes what you say."

And they did just that: After Jesus had died, they talked about him everywhere.

And even though they could not see him, Jesus helped them all the time.

The Gospel of the Lord.

Prayer of the Faithful

God our Father, you sent Jesus, the first missionary, on his great mission. We pray for the friends of Jesus in faraway countries today. Help them to spread the love of Jesus around the world, and to help everyone to be friends.

1. We pray for priests who work around the world. Be with them as they work. Lord, hear us. R.

2. We pray for sisters who work around the world. Be with them as they work. Lord, hear us. R.

3. We pray for lay people who work around the world. Be with them as they work. Lord, hear us. R.

4. We pray for people around the world who do not know about Jesus. Be with them as they work. Lord, hear us. R.

5. We pray for children around the world who do not know about Jesus. Be with them as they work. Lord, hear us. R.

Preparation of the Gifts

1. We bring a lighted candle. We help people to be friends of Jesus.

2. We bring a globe. We help everyone in the world to be friends together.

3. We bring our mission boxes. We help especially by sharing what we have.

4. We bring our lives to God, with the bread and wine.

Second Prayer

God our Father, we bring you our gifts of bread and wine. With them, we bring ourselves, and our brothers and sisters around the world. Take us all in the name of Jesus Christ, your Son, who lives and reigns with you in the unity of the Holy Spirit, one God forever and ever. Amen.

Third Prayer

God our Father, may this holy communion help us to love each other and to love our brothers and sisters around the world. We make our prayer through Jesus Christ, your Son, who lives and reigns with you in the unity of the Holy Spirit, one God forever and ever. Amen.

Final Blessing

Go in peace, to love God, and to help and share with your brothers and sisters around the world.

17. God Knows Me

The theme of this Mass is the "specialness" of each one of us. God has made each one of us so special and so different. And yet God knows every one of us, and knows everything about every one of us. God knows us even by our very own names.

First Prayer

God our Father, we thank you for the "specialness" of each one of us. Help us to know, love, and thank you always for making us your very special children. We make our prayer through Jesus Christ, your Son, who lives and reigns with you in the unity of the Holy Spirit, one God forever and ever. Amen.

First Reading Genesis 1:24–31

Then God said:

Let us make people—and he made men and women and put them in charge of the world.

Then God looked at everything, and God said: "It is all very good!"

The Word of the Lord.

Responsorial Psalm Psalm 138:1-11

This is a song of praise to God the Father who loves us too much to leave us all on our own.

RESPONSE: You are always close to us, O Lord.

1. You know me Lord, so very well.

You know when I get up.

You know when I go back to sleep.

You know each thing I do. R.

2. You know what I am going to say, even before I speak!

You are always close to me.

You're wonderful, O Lord. R.

3. So if I climbed the highest hill,

you would be there with me.
And if I swam beneath the waves,
you'd still be there with me. R.
4. Even in the dark at night
you would be next to me.
Yes, even then I would not hide,
you would be there with me. R.

Second Reading Colossians 3:12, 16, 17
St. Paul tells us in this reading that God wants to get to know us because God loves us.

Dear friends,
Don't forget that God wants to get to know you, because God loves you. But you must help each other to know how much God loves you by singing God's songs.

And remember! When you sing these songs, say "thank you" to God for God is your Father in heaven.
The Word of the Lord.

Gospel Acclamation
Alleluia, alleluia,
I know all my sheep, everyone of them, and they know me.
Alleluia.

Gospel John 10:3-5, 14
God looks after us like a shepherd, and he knows us. Jesus looks after us like a shepherd as well, and he knows each of us—even our names.

One day, Jesus said:
Sheep listen to their own shepherd and they will follow him.

He can even call them one by one, for he knows their names and he can call them out of the sheepfold through the gate. When they have all come out, he walks in front of them, and they all follow because they know the sound of his voice.

Of course, they would never follow a stranger because they would not know the sound of his voice. They would run away from him if he told them to follow him.

Then Jesus said:

I am a shepherd and I am a good shepherd. I know all my sheep, every one of them, and they know me.

The Gospel of the Lord.

Prayer of the Faithful

God our Father, we your children, gathered here around your table, bring to you in prayer our own needs and the needs of people far and near.

1. We pray for our fathers and mothers, and for parents all around the world. Bless them and help them to know you. Lord, hear us. R.

2. We pray for our brothers and sisters, and for brothers and sisters all around the world. Bless them and help them to know you. Lord, hear us. R.

3. We pray for young people in our parish, and for young people all around the world. Bless them and help them to know you. Lord, hear us. R.

4. We pray for old people in our parish, and for the elderly all around the world. Bless them and help them to know you. Lord, hear us. R.

5. We pray for children with special needs in our parish, and for children with special needs all around the world. Bless them and help them to know you. Lord, hear us. R.

6. We pray for children who are fearful, lonely, and treated badly in our parish and all around the world. Bless them and help them to know you. Lord, hear us. R.

Preparation of the Gifts

1. We bring a lump of clay. We are like the clay, and God is the potter who molds the clay.

2. We bring a list of our names. Each of us is special and different, and God knows us by our own names.

3. We bring our lives to God, with the bread and wine.

Second Prayer

God our Father, we bring you our gifts and we bring you the "specialness" of each one of us here today. Bless us all and help us to know you. We make this prayer through Jesus Christ, your Son, who lives and reigns with you in the unity of the Holy Spirit, one God forever and ever. Amen.

Third Prayer

God our Father, Jesus is with us in this holy communion. May he help us to remember our own "specialness," and may he help us to let you continue to mold us like the potter who molds the clay. We make this prayer through Jesus Christ, your Son, who lives and reigns with you in the unity of the Holy Spirit, one God forever and ever. Amen.

Final Blessing

Go in peace, to know God, and to love God.

18. Family

The theme of this Mass is the family. We thank God for our families. We thank God especially for our father and mother, who show us God's love and care in our families.

First Prayer

God our Father, we thank you for our family. Thank you for fathers, mothers, brothers, and sisters. Make us glad to be together and help us to love you more. We ask this through Jesus, your Son, who lives and reigns with you in the unity of the Holy Spirit, one God forever and ever. Amen.

First Reading Ezekiel 36:24-28

In this reading we are reminded that we are all God's children and that we all belong to God's family.

God says:

I want all my people to come back to me and live at home with me again. Your hearts have become hard as stone, but I will make you kind and you will do what I will tell you, for I will give you my Holy Spirit. I will pour water over you and wash all the dirt away, so that you may be clean all over. You will be my family and I will be your father.

The Word of the Lord.

Responsorial Psalm Psalm 99:1-5

This is a poem that says thank you to God, because we know God is so interested in us, the children of God.

RESPONSE: We thank you, we praise you for you are good and loving.

1. Let everyone be happy,

Let everyone be glad,

Let everyone be full of joy

and sing to the Lord. R.

2. We know the Lord is God
who gives us life and breath,
for we are God's own family
and we belong to him. R.

Second Reading Romans 12:8, 10, 11, 13
This reading is from one of the letters of St. Paul. It tells us that God our Father wants us to love, like Jesus.

Dear friends,
God is making things better all the time.
God knows all the people who love God, and gives them each a job to do so that they can work with God.
God wants us all to become more like Jesus, his Son,
for Jesus is our eldest brother in the family of God.
The Word of the Lord.

Gospel Acclamation
Alleluia, alleluia.
You will all be my brothers and my sisters as well,
if you do what God wants you to do.
Alleluia.

Gospel Mark 3:20, 21, 3 1-35
This reading tells us that, if we do what God wants us to do, we are God's brothers, sisters, and mother as well.

One day, Jesus went home and so many people came to see him and he was so busy that he didn't even have time to eat anything.

When his family heard about this, they said he was mad, and they came along to help him. But there were so many people outside the house they couldn't even get anywhere near him. So they sent him a message, saying, "Your mother and the rest of your family are outside and they want to see you." Inside the house everyone was sit-

ting around Jesus in a circle, and he looked around at them all and said, "You will all be my brothers and sisters and my mother as well, if you do what God wants you to do."
The Gospel of the Lord.

Prayer of the Faithful

We thank you God for all your love and goodness. We pray for the needs of all parents and their children.

1. Bless all our parents. Help them to lead their children to you, by word and example. Lord, hear us. R.

2. Bless all of us, your children. Help us to grow daily in your love. Lord, hear us. R.

3. Bless all the parents in this parish. Help them to love and care for their children. Lord, hear us. R.

4. Bless all the children in this parish. Help them always to love and obey their parents. Lord, hear us. R.

5. Bless the families of the whole world. Fill them with your love and happiness. Lord, hear us. R.

6. We pray for our friends who have died. Give them eternal rest in their heavenly home. Lord, hear us. R.

Preparation of the Gifts

1. We bring a bible. Our family grows together in faith.
2. We bring a rosary beads. Our family grows together in love.
3. We bring our lives to God, with the bread and wine.

Second Prayer

God our Father, we bring you our gifts of bread and wine. With them, we bring the love and goodness of our family. Help us all to grow in our love for you and for each other. We make our prayer through Jesus, your Son, who lives and reigns with you in the unity of the Holy Spirit, one God forever and ever. Amen.

Third Prayer

God our Father, we have come close to your Son in this communion. Help us to come close to each other in our family. We make our prayer through Jesus, your Son, who lives and reigns with you in the unity of the Holy Spirit, one God forever and ever. Amen.

Final Blessing

Go in peace, to love and thank God for all God's love and goodness. Amen.

19. Friends Are a Gift

The theme of this Mass is friends. A faithful friend is one of the best gifts that God has given us. We are very lucky to have friends around us—to play with, to talk to, and to help us. Today we think of all of our friends and we thank God for them. We thank God, too, for the happiness we can have with them.

First Prayer
God our Father, we thank you for our friends. Help us to be true friends to each other and to love one another like real friends. We make our prayer through Jesus, your Son, who lives and reigns with you in the unity of the Holy Spirit, one God forever and ever. Amen.

First Reading Philippians 3:8, 10
St. Paul is telling us in this reading that Jesus is a great friend to have, especially when we feel sad or sorry for ourselves. We can be sure that Jesus will always understand our troubles and that he will be a real friend to us.

Dear friends,
Nothing could be better than knowing Jesus!
I would give up everything, just to stay friends with him.
Remember how much he suffered, and don't forget that we can always share our troubles with him, when things go wrong.
The Word of the Lord.

Responsorial Psalm Psalm 62:7-9
This is a song of praise to God for God's love, care and friendship at all times.
RESPONSE: Lord God, I am happy to be with you.
1. At night, I lie in bed and think of you, Lord God. R.
2. I lie there in the darkness of the night and remember how good you are, for you have always helped me. R.
3. I am like a little bird that clings to its mother. R.
4. You are like the mighty eagle who spreads its wings above its

young to protect them. R.
5. I am happy to lie here in the dark under the shadow of your wings, Lord God. R.

Gospel Acclamation
Alleluia, alleluia.
I want you to be my friends and be happy with me.
Alleluia.

Gospel John 15:15-17
St. John is telling us in this reading that Jesus wants us to be his friends. He doesn't want us just to work for him.

One day Jesus said: "I don't want you just to work for me and do as you're told. I want you to be my friends and be happy with me.
"But remember, you did not choose me; I chose you to be my friends and I want you to be friends with each other."
The Gospel of the Lord.

Prayers of the Faithful
God our Father, you are the special friend of little children. You said to your friends, "Don't stop the children from coming to me. Bring them back." Put your arms around us now and bless us as we pray.
1. Bless our fathers and mothers. Help us to be real friends together. Lord, hear us. R.
2. Bless all of us, your children, as we work, play, and pray together. Help us to be real friends together. Lord, hear us. R.
3. Bless the children who are lonely, forgotten, and without friends. Help us to be real friends together. Lord, hear us. R.
4. Bless the children who are unhappy because they have no friends. Help us to be real friends together. Lord hear us. R.
5. Bless the children around the world who are cold, hungry and unhappy. Help us to be real friends together. Lord hear us. R.
Preparation of the Gifts
1. We bring some flowers. We give flowers to friends.

2. We bring a globe. We remember our friends around the world.

3. We bring our lives to God, with the bread and wine.

Second Prayer

God our Father, we, your friends, bring to you now ourselves and all our friends. Bless us all and put your loving arms around us. We make this prayer through Jesus Christ, your Son, who lives and reigns with you in the unity of the Holy Spirit, one God forever and ever. Amen.

Communion Litany

RESPONSE: Thank you, God, for friends.

1. For friends who talk to me,

And for friends who share with me. R.

2. For friends who play with me,

And for friends who help me. R.

3. For friends who comfort me,

And for friends who cheer me up when I'm sad. R.

4. For friends who are kind to me,

And for friends who tell me the truth about myself. R.

5. For friends who understand me,

And for friends who make me happy. R.

Third Prayer

God our Father, you have given us Jesus our friend, in this holy communion. Help us to be his friends forever and ever. We make this prayer through Jesus, your Son, who lives and reigns with you in the unity of the Holy Spirit, one God forever and ever. Amen.

Final Blessing

Go in peace, to love God, and always be God's friend.

20. Hands

The theme of this Mass is hands. Our hands are very important—we need them to do everything. We need them to do things for ourselves—playing, dressing, eating, feeling, and writing. We need them to do things for others—sharing, giving, holding, lifting, and helping. We will think about the best ways to use our hands.

First Prayer

God our Father, we thank you for our hands.

We thank you for what we can do with them.

Help us to use them in kind and helpful ways.

We ask this through Jesus, your Son, who lives and reigns with you in the unity of the Holy Spirit, one God forever and ever. Amen.

First Reading

This is the story of Mother Teresa of Calcutta. It is the story of a very kind and generous woman, who uses her hands to help.

Mother Teresa lives in India, in a big city called Calcutta. When she became a nun, she felt called to work in the very poor parts of that city. She went to the slums and taught the poor children. She loved them and cared for them.

She visited the sick and helped them.

She saw many poor people dying on the streets.

She asked the mayor of Calcutta for help to set up a home for them. She wanted those dying people to know and to feel that they were wanted. She wanted them to know that they were loved. She wanted them to know that they were God's children and that God would never forget them and would never leave them. Mother Teresa still uses her hands to comfort the people of Calcutta. She brings happiness to them, and she brings happiness to people everywhere around the world.

Responsorial Psalm Psalm 15:7-9

This is a prayer of thanks to God, because God keeps us safe in God's hands.

RESPONSE: Lord God, we are safe with you.

1. We praise the Lord, for God guides us along the right path. R.
2. By day and by night God shows us what to do. R.
3. We shall not fall down if God is there beside us. R.
4. Lord, we are happy for we are safe with you. R.

Second Reading   Isaiah 58:7-8

Isaiah is telling us that we must take care of each other.

You must share things. You must feed the hungry, and get houses for the poor people. And you must buy clothes for the people who haven't got enough. If you do this, you will make the whole world bright. You will be like the sun that fills the sky with light each morning.

The Word of the Lord.

Gospel Acclamation

Alleluia, alleluia,

Don't stop the children from coming to me.

Bring them back.

Alleluia.

Gospel Mark 10: 13, 14, 16

Jesus used his hands to do good, to heal and to help. In this story, he uses his hands to welcome the children, and to bless them.

People often used to bring children to Jesus and, when they did, Jesus always gave them his blessing. One day, however, some of the friends of Jesus told the children to go away. Jesus was angry when he saw this happening, and he said: "Don't stop the children from coming to me. Don't send them away like that! Bring them back." Then he put his arms round the children and he blessed them.

The Gospel of the Lord.

Prayer of the Faithful

God our Father, we thank you for people who work for us, and we pray for all those who use their hands to help us.

1. Bless our Pope, our bishop, and our priests, who bring us your love, and forgiveness. Lord, hear us. R.

2. Bless our mothers and fathers, who make our homes warm and loving. Lord, hear us. R.

3. Bless our teachers, who make our schools friendly and happy. Lord, hear us. R.

4. Bless the doctors and the nurses, who help us in sickness. Lord, hear us. R.

5. Bless the farmers and the bakers, who work for our food. Lord, hear us. R.

6. Bless our friends, who are always loving and kind. Lord, hear us. R.

Preparation of the Gifts

1. We bring our best writing, all the work of our hands.
2. We bring our best painting, all the work of our hands.
3. We bring our best handiwork.
4. We bring our lives to God, with the bread and wine.

Second Prayer

God our Father, we bring you our hands, and all the work we do with them. Take them with our gifts of bread and wine. We make this prayer through Jesus, your Son, who lives and reigns with you in the unity of the Holy Spirit, one God forever and ever. Amen.

Communion Litany

RESPONSE: We thank you, Lord our God.
1. For kind hands that help at home
And for kind hands that help at school. R.
2. For kind hands that bless and pray
And for kind hands that play happy games. R.

3. For kind hands that share
And for kind hands that give gifts. R.
4. For kind hands that comfort
And for kind hands that stroke gently. R.
5. For kind hands that make beautiful things
And for kind hands that enjoy things. R.

Third Prayer

God our Father, Jesus is with us now. He used his hands to comfort, to console, to bless, and to help. May we use our hands like Jesus. We ask this through Jesus Christ, your Son, who lives and reigns with you in the unity of the Holy Spirit, one God forever and ever. Amen.

Blessing of Hands

A simple ceremony of blessing of hands may take place before the final blessing.

Final Blessing

Go in peace, to know God, and to love God.

21. Speaking

Today we are thinking about speaking and about the ways God wants us to use this wonderful gift to make people happy.

First Prayer
God our Father, thank you for the gift of speaking. Help us to use our voices to bring happiness to others. We ask this through Jesus, your Son, who lives and reigns with you in the unity of the Holy Spirit, one God forever and ever. Amen.

First Reading Lev iticus 19:16-18
This reading comes from the Book of Moses. It tells us how God wants us to use our voices.

God says:
You must not tell lies about other people. You must not hate anyone.
   If someone has done wrong, tell them that they have done wrong, but don't try to get revenge.
   Don't grumble, either. You must take care of each other just as much as you take care of yourself.
The Word of the Lord.

Responsorial Psalm Psalm 27:6-7
The responsorial psalm is taken from the Book of Praise. We tell God we know we can always trust him.
RESPONSE: Blessed be God.
1. God listens to me. God hears me when I pray for help. R.
2. I trust the Lord for the Lord is strong. R.
3. I thank the Lord for the Lord takes care of me. R.

Second Reading James 3:5, 6, 9
This reading is from one of the letters of St. James. He gives us good advice

about using the gift of speaking.

The tongue is like a little flame, friendly and warm. But just as a little flame can start a forest fire, the tongue can do very great harm by telling lies and saying unkind things.

My friends: The tongue speaks your voice. It is holy. It is from God. Always use it to give praise to God.

The Word of the Lord.

Gospel Acclamation

Alleluia, alleluia,

I want to sing and to shout because I am so happy.

Alleluia.

Gospel Luke 17:11-16

This reading is from the Gospel of St. Luke. It is the story of the man who said, "thank you" to Jesus. It shows us that we must never forget to say "thank you."

One day, Jesus went up to Jerusalem and, while he was on his way, he went into a little town nearby.

Ten lepers came out to meet him there, and they waved across to him, saying, "Please help us, Jesus!"

When he saw them, Jesus said, "Go and see the priest!" So they did and, as they were on their way, they were healed!

One of the ten came right back to Jesus and he praised God at the top of his voice, throwing himself down in front of Jesus. "Thank you, Jesus," he said, "Thank you very much!"

The Gospel of the Lord.

Prayer of the Faithful

God our Father, we thank you for all your gifts, especially the gift of speaking. We pray for all those who use this gift to make you better known and loved.

1. We pray for our Holy Father, Pope John Paul, who often speaks to us about God's love. Lord, hear us. R.

2. We pray for our mothers and fathers who tell us about God's love. Lord, hear us. R.

3. We pray for our priests and teachers who pass on God's message of love in school. Lord, hear us. R.

4. We pray for missionaries who spread God's message of love in faraway countries. Lord, hear us. R.

5. We pray for all those who speak out bravely for justice and peace. Lord, hear us. R.

6. We thank you for the gift of speaking. We pray for people with speech difficulties. Lord, hear us. R.

Preparation of the Gifts

1. We bring a Bible for God's spoken word.
2. We bring a newspaper for everyday news.
3. We bring a radio for news, views, and music.
4. We bring our lives to God, with the bread and wine.

Second Prayer

God our Father, we give you ourselves with these gifts of bread and wine. Help us always to use our voices well—to praise you, to offer help, to give comfort, and to say "thanks." We make our prayer through Jesus, your Son, who lives and reigns with you in the unity of the Holy Spirit, one God forever and ever. Amen.

Third Prayer

God our Father, your Son Jesus is with us now. May he stay with us always and help us to bring peace and joy to everybody. We make this prayer through Jesus, your Son, who lives and reigns with you in the unity of the Holy Spirit, one God forever and ever. Amen.

Final Blessing

Go in peace, to love God, and to praise God with your voice.

22. The Gift of Seeing

Today we thank God for our eyes—eyes that can see so many wonders around us. Most of all we are glad that we can see people who are good, kind, and always loving.

First Prayer

God our Father, thank you for the gift of seeing. As we look at your lovely world, help us to praise you. We make this prayer through Jesus Christ, your Son, who lives and reigns with you in the unity of the Holy Spirit, one God forever and ever. Amen.

First Reading

The reading is a poem of thanks that we can see beautiful things —flowers, trees, and people we love.

All things bright and beautiful
All creatures great and small
All things wise and wonderful
The Lord God made them all.
He gave us eyes to see them
And lips that we might tell
How great is God Almighty
Who has made all things well.

Responsorial Psalm Psalm 148:3, 7-13.
This is a lovely song of praise to God for everything. We join in praise of God, too.
RESPONSE: Let everyone praise God.
1. The sun and the moon praise God, the shining stars adore God. Snow and hail praise God, and the mighty winds that obey God. R.
2. The depths of the sea praise God, and all the monsters of the ocean. The birds in the sky praise God, and even the snakes that crawl on the ground. R.

---

3. All the animals of the world praise God, both wild and tame. The hills and mountains praise God, and all the trees. R.

Second Reading Revelation 15:3-4
Jesus wants us to praise God for all God has done for us.

Lord God, how great you are. Everything you have done is wonderful. You are the King of the whole wide world. Who will not praise you! Who will not thank you! You are God, the Holy one! Everyone will come and worship you, for everyone can see what you have done.
The Word of the Lord.

Gospel Acclamation
Alleluia, alleluia.
Jesus said: "You know that I am alive, because you can see me."
Alleluia.

Gospel Matthew 6:22-33
Jesus is telling us to be clear-eyed, to see things as he sees them.

Your eye is the lamp of your body. If your eyesight is good, you can see the whole world clearly; if your eyesight is bad, you can't see anything clearly; if you are really blind, how dark it is.
The Gospel of the Lord.

Prayer of the Faithful
God our Father, you help us to see goodness in everyone. We ask you to be with us now as we pray.
1. Help us to see the goodness and beauty of God, in the lovely world around us.
Response: Lord, that we may see.
2. Help us to see the love and goodness of others.
Response: Lord, that we may see.

3. Help us to see when our help is needed, at home and in school.

Response: Lord, that we may see.

4. Help us to see, and respond, to the needs of the sick and old people in our area.

Response: Lord, that we may see.

5. Help us to see when people are doing their best for us.

Response: Lord, that we may see.

Preparation of the Gifts

1. We bring a colorful plant. We see God's goodness in the world.

2. We bring a lighted candle. Jesus helps us to see how we should live.

3. We bring our lives to God, with the bread and wine.

Second Prayer

God our Father, we bring you our gifts. Help us to see your daily gifts, signs of your love and goodness to us. We make this prayer through Jesus Christ, your Son, who lives and reigns with you in the unity of the Holy Spirit, one God forever and ever. Amen.

Communion Litany

RESPONSE: Lord God, we praise and thank you.

1. For eyes to see and admire God's wonderful world. R.

2. For eyes to see the love and goodness of our mothers and fathers. R.

3. For eyes to love and help at home. R.

4. For eyes to see people in need, and to help them. R.

5. For eyes to share, and to give to others. R.

6. For eyes full of love, kindness, and compassion for those in need of comfort and sympathy. R.

7. For eyes, to make our friends happy. R.

8. For eyes, ever ready to do a good turn. R.

Third Prayer

God our Father, may the coming of Jesus in holy communion help us to see your love and goodness in our lives. We make this prayer through Jesus Christ, your Son, who lives and reigns with you in the unity of the Holy Spirit, one God forever and ever. Amen.

Final Blessing

Go in peace, to love God, and see the lovely things he has given us.

23. Happiness

The theme is happiness. Many people work for our happiness—helping, making, serving, and giving. We thank God for the people in our lives who work for our happiness. We, in turn, try to make others happy.

First Prayer
God our Father, thank you for all the happiness we enjoy in our homes and at school. Help us always to wear a happy smile, so that those who see us may feel happy, too. We make this prayer through Jesus Christ, your Son, who lives and reigns with you in the unity of the Holy Spirit, one God forever and ever. Amen.

First Reading Sirach 11:8-10
God wants us to be happy people, and to enjoy ourselves.

It is wonderful to see the brightness of the sunshine.
It is good to enjoy ourselves all through our lives,
and especially when we are young.
There's so much to do!
There's so much to see!
May you always be healthy.
May you never be sad.
The Word of the Lord.

Responsorial Psalm Psalm 99:1-5
God is good and loving. God wants us to be happy. We praise and thank God.
RESPONSE: We praise you, Lord.
1. Let everyone be happy.
Let everyone be glad.
Let everyone be full of joy and sing to the Lord our God. R.
2. We know the Lord is God.
God gives us life and breath,

for we are God's own family and we belong to God. R.
3. We thank you, Lord.
We praise you, Lord,
For you are good and loving. R.

Gospel Acclamation
Alleluia, alleluia.
Jesus said:
"I want you to be happy with me."
Alleluia.

Gospel John 15:15-16
The reading is from the Gospel of St. John. He tells us that Jesus wants us to be his friends and to be happy.

One day, Jesus said:
I don't want you just to work for me and do as you're told. I want you to be my friends and be happy with me!
The Gospel of the Lord.

Prayer of the Faithful
As we think today about happiness, we want it for ourselves, and we want it for those we love. We pray that God will help us to spread the happiness that Jesus came to give us all.
1. Help us to spread happiness at home, by our pleasant words and happy faces. Lord, hear us. R.
2. Help us to spread happiness at home, by helping whenever we can. Lord, hear us. R.
3. Help us to spread happiness at school, by doing our work well. Lord, hear us. R.
4. Help us to spread happiness at school, by being gentle and kind with our friends. Lord, hear us. R.
5. Help us to spread happiness in the playground, by letting others join in our games. Lord, hear us. R.

Preparation of the Gifts
1. We bring a dust cloth. We spread happiness at home when we help.
2. We bring a storybook. We spread happiness at school when we work well.
3. We bring a ball. We spread happiness at play when we let others join in our games.
4. We bring our lives to God, with the bread and wine.

Second Prayer
God our Father, we bring you our gifts of bread and wine. With these gifts, we bring the happiness we feel and the things you give to make us happy. We make this prayer through Jesus Christ, your Son, who lives and reigns with you in the unity of the Holy Spirit, one God forever and ever. Amen.

Communion Litany
RESPONSE: Thank you, God.
1. For loving parents, and our happy homes. R.
2. For caring teachers, and our happy schools. R.
3. For the cheerful, happy smiles of friends. R.
4. For pleasant words and praise from others. R.
5. For the helping, sharing, and giving of friends. R.
6. For happy outings, treats, and jokes. R.
7. For the food we eat, and for all God's gifts to us. R.
8. For happy times together on holidays and weekends. R.

Third Prayer
God our Father, we give thanks for Jesus who has taught us how to be happy, and how to make others happy. We will try to make our world the happy place he would like it to be. We make this prayer through

Jesus Christ, your Son, who lives and reigns with you in the unity of the Holy Spirit, one God forever and ever. Amen.

Final Blessing
Go in peace, to love God, and spread happiness wherever you are.

24. Gladness and Joy

Today we think about the gifts of gladness and joy. We celebrate our feelings of gladness and joy. We thank God for all the things in our lives that give us great joy and gladness, and make us so happy.

First Prayer
God our Father, we thank you for our gladness and joy. Help us to share our joy with others, at all times and in all seasons. We make this prayer through Jesus Christ, your Son, who lives and reigns with you in the unity of the Holy Spirit, one God forever and ever. Amen.

First Reading Isaiah 12:4-6
The reading comes from a wise man called Isaiah. It's a song of joy because God is so good.

I want to tell the whole wide world—"God has been good to me!"
I want to tell the whole wide world—"God is wonderful!"
I want to sing and to shout because I am so happy, for God has come to me and God is great!
The Word of the Lord.

Responsorial Psalm Psalm 46:2-3, 6-8
This is a song of joy and praise to God, King of all the earth.
RESPONSE: Clap your hands and shout for joy.
1. Clap your hands and shout for joy. God is King of all the earth! R.
2. Play the trumpet loud and clear. God is King of all the earth! R.
3. Sing and praise God, everyone. God is King of all the earth! R.
4. Praise God now with all your skill. God is King of all the earth! R.

Second Reading Colossians 3:16-17
St. Paul tells us our hearts should be full of songs of joy and praise and love.

Dear friends,

How full of songs your hearts will be, songs of joy and praise and love, songs to God! In this spirit, you can take everything in your stride, matching word and deed, as the friends of the Lord Jesus. Make Jesus the center of your life; and with his help let your hearts be filled with thankfulness to God—your Father.

The Word of the Lord.

Gospel Acclamation

Alleluia, alleluia.

Jesus said:

"Father, I want to share my joy to the full with all those you have given to me."

Alleluia

Gospel Matthew 5:3-10

Jesus tells us we will be happy if we do what God wants, if we forgive and if we help people to be friends.

How happy are you, if you are poor!
God will make you rich!
How happy are you, if you are not very important!
God will make you great!
How happy are you if you desire to do what God wants!
God will see that you get what you want as well!
How happy are you, if you forgive others!
God will forgive you!
How happy are you, if you really want to know God!
God will make sure you get to know God well!
How happy are you, if you help people to be friends!
God will be friends with you!
How happy are you, if people attack you!
especially when you are trying to do what God wants
God will welcome you with open arms.

The Gospel of the Lord.

Prayer of the Faithful
God our Father, you want everyone to be joyful and happy in the world. We pray that you will fill us all with joy and gladness today, and help us to share this joy and gladness to the full, with others.
1. Give joy to us, and to all our families. Help us to know that you are always with us. Lord, hear us. R.
2. Give joy to all our friends. Help them to know that you are always near, and never far from them. Lord, hear us. R.
3. Give joy to all who work to spread peace in our homes, in our schools, in our parish, in our country. Help them to know that you are beside them, helping in their work. Lord, hear us. R.
4. Give joy to those who are sick. Help them to know that you love them, and remember them. Lord, hear us. R.
5. Give joy to those who are sad and unhappy, because someone they loved has died. Help them to know that you care for them. Lord, hear us. R.

Preparation of the Gifts
1. We bring flowers. Flowers give joy to all of us.
2. We bring balloons. Balloons are a sign of our joy today.
3. We bring some toys. Toys give joy and happiness.
4. We bring our lives to God, with the bread and wine.

Second Prayer
God our Father, we bring you our gifts of bread and wine. With them, we bring all the gladness and joy of our lives. We make this prayer through Jesus Christ, your Son, who lives and reigns with you in the unity of the Holy Spirit, one God forever and ever. Amen.

Communion Litany
RESPONSE: Lord, we thank you.
1. For our parents and families, who love and who share. R.

2. For friends who remember us, and show that they care. R.

3. For our schools and our teachers, who show us the way. R.

4. For our church and our priests, who lead us in prayer. R.

5. For the beauty around us, to see and enjoy. R.

6. For our food that is fresh, with plenty to spare. R.

7. For our health and our homes, and the happy times there. R.

8. For songs and for games, to enjoy and to play. R.

Third Prayer

God our Father, each day you continue to show signs of your love and goodness. Stay with us, as we share our joy and gladness with those we meet today. We make this prayer through Jesus Christ, your Son, who lives and reigns with you in the unity of the Holy Spirit, one God forever and ever. Amen.

Final Blessing

Go in peace, to love and serve God, with gladness and joy.

25. God's Colorful World

Today we are thinking about our colorful world. We see color everywhere. We have spring and summer colors, autumn and winter colors. We give thanks to God for this gift of color that makes the world so beautiful.

First Prayer

God our Father, we thank you for this beautiful, colorful world. May its color help us to know and love you. We make our prayer through Jesus, your Son, who lives and reigns with you in the unity of the Holy Spirit, one God forever and ever. Amen.

First Reading

This reading is about the color green. It is a prayer of thanks and praise to God, the greatest artist.

We praise you, Lord.
You have given us many lovely colors.
Green is one of those special colors—
You have painted many shades of green.
You have made our countryside
colurful and beautiful—
with green fields and green meadows,
with green hills and green valleys.
You know, Lord, that green
is soft and soothing.
It is relaxing and refreshing.
Green does not tire our eyes.
Green gives us life.
Green gives us hope.
Thank you, God, for the color green.

Responsorial Psalm Psalm 104
RESPONSE: God is great, God is wonderful.

1. Lord God, how great you are.
Everything you have done is wonderful.
You are the king of the whole wide world. R.
2. Who will not praise you! Who will not thank you! R.
3. Everyone will come and worship you,
for everyone can see what you have done. R.

Second Reading Revelation 4:2-4,6
This reading is from the last book of the Bible. St. John tells us that heaven, too, is bright and beautiful and full of color.

I saw a throne standing in heaven, and the person sitting there looked like a diamond and a ruby. There was a rainbow encircling the throne and this looked like an emerald.

Around the throne in a circle were twenty-four thrones, and on them I saw twenty-four elders sitting, dressed in white robes with golden crowns on their heads.

Between the throne and myself was a sea that seemed to be made of glass, like crystal.
The Word of the Lord.

Gospel Acclamation
Alleluia, alleluia.
God looked at everything and God said
"It is all very good!"
Alleluia.

Gospel John 4:35-36
This reading is from the Gospel of St. John. It tells us that Jesus knew that the world was good and beautiful, especially at harvest time.

One day, Jesus said:
Everything is going just right!
There's going to be a marvelous harvest.
Isn't it wonderful!

One man sows the seed
And three months later the field is full of golden corn,
ready for the harvest.
Then another man comes and cuts down the corn
and stores it in the barns.
And everyone is happy together.
The Gospel of the Lord.

Prayer of the Faithful

God our Father, you are great. You have given us many different colors. We thank and praise you, and we pray:

1. Help us to see your greatness in the colorful world you have given us. Lord, hear us. R.

2. Help us to know your goodness when we see signs of your love in the world about us. Lord, hear us. R.

3. Help us to be thankful for the good and beautiful things you give us. Lord, hear us. R.

4. Help us to love and care for each other as you care for even the smallest plants and animals. Lord, hear us. R.

5. Help us, like the trees and the flowers, to grow up toward you in love. Lord, hear us. R.

Preparation of the Gifts

1. We bring red apples.
2. We bring green leaves.
3. We bring yellow daffodils.
4. We bring blue flowers.
5. We bring our lives to God, with the bread and the wine.

Second Prayer

God our Father, we bring you ourselves with the bread and the wine. We bring you all the color in our world. We make this prayer through Jesus, your Son, who lives and reigns with you, in the unity of the Holy Spirit, one God forever and ever.

Communion Litany

RESPONSE: Lord our God, we praise and thank you.

1. We thank you for the rainbow that brightens the sky. R.
2. We thank you for the golden sun. R.
3. We thank you for the colors of the clouds in the vast blue sky. R.
4. We thank you for all the different shades of green. R.
5. We thank you for the silvery lakes and the shining sea. R.
6. We thank you for the brown bog and the purple heather. R.
7. We thank you for the bright flowers and the glossy leaves. R.

Third Prayer

God our Father, may this holy communion help us to grow in your love in this colorful world, and lead us to you. We make our prayer through Jesus, your Son, who lives.

Final Blessing

Go in peace, to love God, and to see the beautiful things God has made.

26. God's Gift of Water

Today we are thinking about God's gift of water. It gives us a lot of enjoyment, and it is very necessary too. When we think about it, we think about God's greatness.

First Prayer
God our Father, you have given us this important gift of water. May it help us to know you and your work better. We ask this through Jesus, your Son, who lives and reigns with you in the unity of the Holy Spirit, one God forever and ever. Amen.

First Reading Psalm 64:10-14
This reading is a song praising God for the gift of water which gives life to everything.

You are the one who sends down the early rain to prepare the soil for the seeds.

You are the one who gathers rain into the rivers to carry water to the crops.

You are the one who gives us gentle showers to soak into the hard-ploughed fields, to soften the earth and make the plants sprout and grow.
The Word of the Lord.

Responsorial Psalm
The Responsorial Psalm is about the wonders of water. We praise God for water that is so useful, and we thank God for this gift that gives us so much enjoyment and so much pleasure.
RESPONSE: Bless the Lord our God.
1. For the beauty of water, bless the Lord. For water that shines and reflects, bless the Lord. R.
2. For the gushing sound of a waterfall, bless the Lord. For the tapping sound of the rain, bless the Lord. R.

3. For shining lakes and flowing rivers, bless the Lord. For rushing brooks and roaring waves, bless the Lord. R.

4. For cool water to quench our thirst, bless the Lord. For water that gives life and growth, bless the Lord. R.

5. For water that washes and cleans, bless the Lord. For water that gives power, bless the Lord. R.

6. For the waters of Baptism, bless the Lord. R.

Second Reading Exodus 15:22-25, 27

This reading is from a Book of Moses. When Moses and the People of God were on their way to the Promised Land, they had to cross the desert and everything became hot and sandy. Then they ran out of water.

They walked for three whole days until they had used up all their water. But when they looked for some more water, they could only find a pool where the water was too horrible to drink.

Everyone grumbled at Moses and said, "What are we going to drink now?" So Moses asked God to help him, and God did not let him down.

Moses found a special kind of wood that he could put into the water to make it nice to drink again. Then everyone could have as much water as they wanted.

Not very long afterwards, they came to a place where there were lots of palm trees and seven pools of clean drinking water, and so they pitched their tents there and set up camp.

The Word of the Lord.

Gospel Acclamation

Alleluia, alleluia.

Lord, you are really the Savior of the world.

Give me the living water, so that I may never get thirsty.

Alleluia.

Gospel John 4:3, 6-8, 27-28

This reading is from the Gospel of St. John. In this story, Jesus and his friends were very thirsty, but they couldn't drink any water, because it was right down at the bottom of a deep well.

One day, Jesus and his friends had to go from Judea to Galilee. They walked all through the morning until they were tired. Then they came to a place called "Jacob's Well" and stopped there for a rest.

Jesus sat down beside the well outside the town, while his friends went to buy some food and, as he sat there, a woman came along with a jug, to get some water from the well.

Jesus asked this woman for a drink. At first, the woman was surprised that Jesus spoke to her, because she did not know him at all. But they soon began to talk to each other, and they were still talking when the others came back with the food. And she left her jug behind when she went away, so they could all have a drink of water from the well.

The Gospel of the Lord.

Prayer of the Faithful

God our Father, in our world there are so many people in need. Let us pray that they may be safe and happy.

1. We pray for people living in dry lands, who have very little water. Lord, hear us. R.

2. We pray for people who have too much water, and whose homes or lands have been flooded. Lord, hear us. R.

3. We pray for people who do not have enough to eat and drink. Lord, hear us. R.

4. We pray for the sick, especially for our own friends. May our Lady of Lourdes help them to get well. Lord, hear us. R.

Preparation of the Gifts

1. We bring holy water and the Easter candle. God uses water to bring us into his family.

2. We bring a towel and a sponge. Water washes and cleans.

3. We bring a glass of water. Water gives life.

4. We bring our lives to God, with the bread and wine.

Second Prayer
God our Father, we give you these gifts of bread and wine. With them, we give you our whole lives. Help us to share the Good News. We make our prayer through Jesus, your Son, who lives and reigns with you in the unity of the Holy Spirit, one God forever and ever. Amen.

Third Prayer
God our Father, you have given us Jesus in this Mass. Help us to grow in his love. We ask this through Jesus, your Son, who lives and reigns with you in the unity of the Holy Spirit, one God forever and ever. Amen.

Blessing the School with Holy Water
God our Father, bless this school. Fill the hearts of your children with goodness. Bless the footsteps of all who come to our school. May every person who comes in be the better for it.

God our Father, bless this room. Bless its four corners. Bless all of us today.

May the blessing of God be upon us all, in the name of the Father, and of the Son, and of the Holy Spirit.

Go in peace, to love God.

27. Light

This theme is about light. Light is very important to us. In the bright summer days we get a lot of light. In the dark winter days we get less light. Light reminds us of Jesus, who was sent to be our light. He is very important to us too, because he is our very special light. He shows us the way to the Father.

First Prayer
God our Father, we thank you for the brightness of light. Thank you, too, for sending us Jesus to be our light. Help us to follow him always. We make our prayer through Jesus, your Son, who lives and reigns with you in the unity of the Holy Spirit, one God forever and ever. Amen.

First Reading Genesis 1:1-3
God knows the importance of light, and how terrible it would be if there was none. So God gave us light.

In the beginning, the world was all empty, and everything was dark and gloomy. But God was there like the wind that blows over the sea. And God said: "Let there be light!" And there was light! And the light was wonderful.
The Word of the Lord.

Responsorial Psalm Psalm 17:2, 4, 29
It is wonderful to be able to see, and we thank God for it. This is a prayer of thanks.
RESPONSE: Lord, you are my light.
1. I love you, my Lord, for you have made me strong. R.
2. I thank you, my Lord, for you have heard my prayer. R.
3. You have been like a light before my eyes. R.
4. You have made my darkness into light. R.

Second Reading 1 John 1: 5-7
St. John tells us that when we do good we walk in God's light, and we stay

close to God.

Dear friends,

God is light! If we do wrong, we turn away from the light of God and go off into the dark.

Some people think they can be close to God and still do wrong. But they are making a mistake!

The light of God shines on us to help us to do things right and be happy with everyone.

The Word of the Lord.

Gospel Acclamation John 7:12

Alleluia, alleluia,

"I am the Light of the World," says the Lord.

"Anyone who follows me will have the light of life."

Alleluia.

Gospel Luke 2:23-32

Simeon and Anna thanked God for letting them see Jesus, "the Light of the World."'

When Jesus was born Joseph and Mary took him to the Temple in Jerusalem, and offered him to God as the Bible told them to do. When they came to the Temple, they met an old man called Simeon. Simeon was a good man and the Holy Spirit was very close to him. And as soon as he saw Jesus, he took him in his arms, and said: "Thank you, God our Father. Now I am happy to die, for I have seen Jesus, the Light of the World!"

The Gospel of the Lord.

Prayer of the Faithful

God our Father, we know you are with us, and that you listen to us. We bring our needs before you now, in prayer.

1. We pray for our Pope, our bishops, and our priests. Be a light to them, and help them as they lead us to you. Lord, hear us. R.

2. We pray for our country. Be a light to our leaders, and bless their work for peace and happiness. Lord, hear us. R.

3. We pray for our families. Be a light to us in our homes, and help us to follow your way of love. Lord, hear us. R.

4. We pray for the children at school. Be a light to us, and help us to live as children of light. Lord, hear us. R.

5. We pray for missionaries. Be a light to them, and help them to bring your light to people in faraway places. Lord, hear us. R.

Preparation of the Gifts
1. We bring a candle. Jesus is our Light.
2. We bring a flashlight and a light bulb. We will walk in the light.
3. We bring our lives to God, with the bread and the wine.

Second Prayer
God our Father, take our gifts of bread and wine. Take our lives, too, and help us to live in the light of Jesus. We ask this through Jesus, your Son, who lives and reigns with you in the unity of the Holy Spirit, one God forever and ever. Amen.

Communion Litany
RESPONSE: We thank you, Lord our God.
1. For Jesus, the Light of the World. R.
2. For the sunlight that brightens our days. R.
3. For the moon and stars that shine in the night. R.
4. For the lightning that shows your splendor and power. R.
5. For the rainbow that colors the sky. R.

Third Prayer
God our Father, you have given us Jesus, our Light. May we follow his way of life, and find true peace and happiness in our lives. We make this prayer through Jesus, your Son, who lives and reigns with you in the unity of the Holy Spirit, one God forever and ever. Amen.

Final Blessing
Go in peace, to love God.

28. Fire

The theme of this Mass is fire. We recall the lovely, cozy, warm feelings we have about fire, and we also remember its power and danger.

First Prayer

God our Father, fire is beautiful, useful, and powerful. It is a gift that reminds us of your love, your power, and your strength. Help us to use it with care and thanks. We make this prayer through Jesus Christ, your Son, who lives and reigns with you in the unity of the Holy Spirit, one God forever and ever. Amen.

First Reading Isaiah 48:14
This is a lovely reading that reminds us about the good and the bad of fire.

It is good to bake bread over a fire. It is good to sit down in front of it and feel warm. But the little fire can blaze up and then no one can bear the heat of its flames, for it can burn people as it they were wisps of straw.
The Word of the Lord.

Responsorial Psalm Psalm 68
This is a psalm of praise to God who is strong, powerful, and mighty.
RESPONSE: Blessed be God.
1.God is … as strong as an earthquake that shakes the whole world and makes the mountains tremble! R.
2. God is … as strong as a volcano that splits the land open, pouring out fire and burning flames and clouds of smoke! R.
3. God is … as powerful as a thunderstorm at night when everything is dark and lightning flashes across the sky, cutting through the heavy rain clouds like an arrow! R.
4. God is … as powerful as a thunderstorm when the mighty sound of thunder rumbles overhead like a deep and angry roar! R.

Gospel Acclamation
Alleluia, alleluia.
Jesus said: "I am like a blazing fire."
Alleluia.

Gospel Luke 12:49
The reading tells us that Jesus is like fire burning strongly so that we can feel his strength and his power.

One day Jesus said: I am like a blazing fire, and I want everyone to feel its heat.
The Gospel of the Lord.

Prayer of the Faithful
God our Father, you are like a fire, powerful, loving, and strong. Listen to our prayers.
1. Help us to be strong, to be kind and loving. Lord, hear us. R.
2. Help us to be strong, with courage to keep on trying. Lord, hear us. R.
3. Help us to be strong, to spread joy and peace. Lord, hear us. R
4. Help us to be strong, to forgive when we are hurt. Lord, hear us. R.
5. Help us to be strong, to comfort those who are lonely and sad. Lord, hear us. R.

Preparation of the Gifts
1. We bring a candle. Fire gives light and brightness.
2. We bring fuel. Fire gives heat, comfort and happiness.
3. We bring a cooking pot. Fire changes food and makes eating enjoyable.
4. We bring our lives to God, with the bread and wine.

Second Prayer
God our Father, we give you our gifts of bread and wine. Take also all the good things that fire can be, and can do for us. We make this

prayer through Jesus Christ, your Son, who lives and reigns with you in the unity of the Holy Spirit, one God forever and ever. Amen.

Litany of Thanks
RESPONSE: Thank you, God.
1. For fire, that brings us together, at home. R.
2. For fire, that comforts, and gives us heat. R.
3. For fire, that crackles, and brightly glows. R.
4. For pleasant fires, to sit around, on dark wintry nights. R.
5. For fireworks, that make a pretty and colorful display. R.
6. For blazing bonfires, that bring us joy and happiness. R.
7. For campfires, that we enjoy in holiday times. R.
8. For the hot sun—the most powerful of all fires. R.

Third Prayer
God our Father, Jesus your Son is with us now. May he stay with us as we try to be warm, loving and kind to those we meet at home, at school, and at play. We make this prayer through Jesus Christ, your Son, who lives and reigns with you in the unity of the Holy Spirit, one God forever and ever. Amen.

Final Blessing
Go in peace, and help everyone to be cheerful and kind.

29. Candles

Today we thank and praise God for his gift of candles. They remind us of pleasant times, such as birthdays and Christmas. They speak to us too of Jesus our light, who came to make our dark world bright.

First Prayer
God our Father, thank you for the gift of candles. They give us light and remind us of Jesus your Son, who came to light up our world of darkness, and lead us to you. We make this prayer through Jesus Christ, your Son, who lives and reigns with you in the unity of the Holy Spirit, one God forever and ever. Amen..

First Reading Isaiah 9:1, 2, 6, 7
This reading comes from the book of a wise man called Isaiah. It tells us that Jesus is like a bright light, showing us the way to the Father.

Once upon a time, everyone lived in the dark, but now—we can see! They used to live in a world that was full of shadows, but now—we have a light to light up our way! We have God with us and God has made us happy.
The Word of the Lord.

Responsorial Psalm Psalm 15:7-9
God our Father guides us and shows us what to do.
RESPONSE: God our Father, we are safe with you.
1. We praise the Lord, for the Lord guides us along the right path. R.
2. By day and by night, the Lord shows us what to do. R.
3. We shall not fall down, if the Lord is there beside us. R.
4. Lord, we are happy, for we are safe with you. R.

Second Reading 1 John 1: 5-7
The reading tells us that, if we follow God's light, we will be happy.

Dear friends,

God is light! If we do wrong, we turn away from the light of God and go off into the dark. Some people think they can be close to God and still do wrong. But they are making a mistake! The light of God shines on us to help us do things right and be happy with everyone. The Word of the Lord.

Gospel Acclamation

Alleluia, alleluia.
Jesus said; "If you are good, you will be like a candle
that shines brightly for everyone to see."
Alleluia.

Gospel Matthew 5:14-15

St. Matthew tells us that, if we are good, we will be like candles showing the way for everyone.

One day, Jesus said: Do you light a candle and then cover it over with a bucket?

Of course you don't! You want it to light up the whole room so that everyone can see.

Then Jesus said: If you are good, you will be like a candle that shines brightly for everyone to see. And if they see that you are good (and they know that you are following God) then they will know that God is good.

The Gospel of the Lord.

Prayer of the Faithful

God our Father, you want us to be like candles, shining brightly for everyone to see. We ask you to help us and our friends to follow you always.

1. Give your light, O Lord, and guide our mothers and fathers as they love and care for us day by day. Lord, hear us. R.

2. Give your light, O Lord, and guide the Pope, bishops, and priests

as they lead us to you. Lord, hear us. R.

3. Give your light, O Lord, and guide the leaders of our country into the way of love and peace. Lord, hear us. R.

4. Give your light, O Lord, and guide our teachers, ourselves, and everybody in our school to learn from each other, and to be a light to one another. Lord, hear us. R.

5. Give your light, O Lord, and guide the people in our parish to show care and concern for people in need. Lord, hear us. R.

Preparation of the Gifts

1. We bring a baptismal candle. In baptism, we are called to follow Jesus, the Light.

2. We bring an Easter candle. At Easter, we renew our promise to follow Jesus, the Light of the World.

3. We bring our lives to God, with the bread and wine.

Second Prayer

God our Father, we bring you gifts of bread and wine. As we bring our candles we ask you to light up our world of darkness and lead us to you. We make this prayer through Jesus Christ, your Son, who lives and reigns with you in the unity of the Holy Spirit, one God forever and ever. Amen.

Communion Litany

RESPONSE: Thank you, God.

1. For our baptism candle, calling us to follow the way of Jesus. R.

2. For birthday candles, small and bright. R.

3. For Christmas candles, often red and colorful. R.

4. For the small church candles, that burn steadily when we go. R.

5. For the tabernacle candles, marking your presence there. R.

6. For prayer candles, marking your presence with us as we pray. R.

7. For the gospel candle, reminding us that you speak to us in the Good News. R.

8. For the Easter candle, which reminds us of Jesus turning darkness into light. R.

Third Prayer
God our Father, Jesus has come to us with his light and love. May we walk in his light and love and be like brightly shining candles for everyone to see. We make this prayer through Jesus Christ, your Son, who lives and reigns with you in the unity of the Holy Spirit, one God forever and ever. Amen.

Final Blessing
Go in peace, to live like Jesus, and to be like a candle that shines brightly for everyone to see.

30. Talents

Today we celebrate the gifts and talents God has given to each one of us. Some of our talents are very obvious, others not so easily seen. But each one of us has the power to use what God has given us, for our own good, and for the good of others.

First Prayer
God our Father, thank you for the talents you have given us. Help us to find out what we can do well, and help us to use our talents generously and usefully. We make this prayer through Jesus Christ, your Son, who lives and reigns with you in the unity of the Holy Spirit, one God forever and ever. Amen.

First Reading Romans 12:6-8
St. Paul is urging us to use our talents and to do everything as well as we can.

Each of us has different talents. God has seen to that. We must use them. For example, some of us are able to understand God's ways more clearly than others; some of us deal with business better; some of us are teachers; some of us are speakers. Let us use our different gifts with God's help. And so with everything we do.

If we give, let us be generous givers; if we are leaders, let us be energetic leaders; if we are helping others, let us be cheerful helpers. The Word of the Lord.

Responsorial Psalm Psalm 138:13-15, 17
We praise God, he does all things well.
RESPONSE: Everything you do is strange and marvelous.
1. Before I was born, you made each little part of me in secret. R.
2. While I was hidden in my mother's womb, you watched me grow. You saw my bones begin to form and join together. R.
3. From the first moment of my life, you knew me. R.
4. I praise you, Lord, and I am filled with wonder. For everything

you do is strange and marvelous. R.

Gospel Acclamation
Alleluia, alleluia.
Jesus said:
"Let your light shine!"
Alleluia.

Gospel Mark 4:21
Jesus wants us to use our talents and all the gifts he has given to us.

Jesus said:
What do you light a lamp for?
To put it out?
To put it under the bed?
Or to put it on the stand to light the whole house and all who live in it?
The Gospel of the Lord.

Prayer of the Faithful
God our Father, we thank you for the gifts and talents you have given to each of us. We pray today that all of us will use our talents, to bring joy and happiness to others—especially to people in need, and those we work with.
1. Lord, bless priests and teachers. Help them to use their gifts of teaching, for the good of all, in our parish and schools. Lord, hear us. R.
2. Lord, bless those who govern our country. Help them to use their gifts to bring peace to our country and to the world. Lord, hear us. R.
3. Lord, bless those people who have plenty. Help them to use their gifts, to help people in need, especially the poor and the hungry. Lord, hear us. R.
4. Lord, bless doctors and nurses, who work for the sick. Help them to use their gifts, to bring healing and comfort to the sick. Lord, hear us. R.

5. Lord, bless us and all other children. Help us to study, to work, to play, to pray, and to bring happiness and joy to all, at home, at school and at play. Lord, hear us. R.

Preparation of the Gifts

1. We bring a tablecloth. We use our gifts, to bring joy and happiness at home.
2. We bring books and pencils. We use our gifts, to bring joy and happiness in school.
3. We bring a ball. We use our gifts at play, to bring joy and happiness.
4. We bring our lives to God, with the bread and wine.

Second Prayer

God our Father, with our gifts of bread and wine, we bring the gifts and talents you have given us. May we always use them for your honor and glory. We make this prayer through Jesus Christ, your Son, who lives and reigns with you in the unity of the Holy Spirit, one God forever and ever. Amen.

Communion Reflection

RESPONSE: Thank you, Lord.

1. For the talent of sport, swimming, running, jumping, and games. R.
2. For the talent of music, singing, playing, and dancing. R.
3. For the talent of art, making, painting, and drawing. R.
4. For the talent of (being good at) knitting, sewing, and cooking. R.
5. For the talent of (being good at) mathematics and science. R.
6. For the talent of being able to see where and when we can help. R.
7. For the talents of gentleness, patience, and kindness. R.
8. For the talent of generosity, and of being always ready to help out. R.

Third Prayer

God our Father, Christ's coming to us has brought us happiness. May we, too, bring happiness to others today, by using our talents to do the best we can. We make this prayer through Jesus Christ, your Son, who lives and reigns with you in the unity of the Holy Spirit, one God forever and ever. Amen.

Final Blessing

Go in peace, to love, and to use all the gifts God has given us.

31. Surprises

The theme of this Mass is surprises. God has given us a world full of surprises. We need only look around and see for ourselves and be generous with our thanks.

First Prayer
God our Father, you give us many surprises. Everyday is a new day and a surprise. Every moment is a surprise from you. Help us always to be glad for everything that happens to us. We make this prayer through Jesus Christ, your Son, who lives and reigns with you in the unity of the Holy Spirit, one God forever and ever. Amen.

First Reading
Every season of the year brings its own surprises, each one fresh and new.

Surprises
I had a surprise last springtime,
I went to the wood one day,
I saw lots of beautiful bluebells,
Looking so bright in May.
I had a surprise last summer,
Walking along the sand,
I found a crab, a baby crab,
and I held it in my hand.
I had a surprise last autumn,
A great big knobbly ball
Fell, with a conker inside it,
Down from the chestnut tall.
I had a surprise last winter,
The world was all shining white,
The snow had covered the garden,
Silently during the night.
Praise God for lovely surprises
God gives us all through the year,

Thank you for eyes to see them,
And memories to hold them dear.

Responsorial Psalm Psalm 95:11-13
This psalm is a song of praise to God for God's wonderful world of surprises.
RESPONSE: Let everything praise God.
1. Let the earth and the sky be glad!
Let the great sea roar!
Let all the fish that swim praise God! R.
2. Let the rich, green fields be happy!
Let the plants and the animals give thanks to the Lord!
Let the trees in the forest shout for joy! R.
3. For God is King. God is King.
God is the Lord of all the world. R.

Second Reading Acts 28:1-3, 10
In this story we hear how St. Paul, too, had some surprises in his travels.

Dear friends,
When we had all reached the beach, we found out where we were—the Island of Malta. The natives didn't treat us as we expected, but showed us every kindness.

It was beginning to rain and everybody was very cold; so they lit a bonfire and made us all feel at home.

The chief of the island welcomed us and looked after us for three days in a most friendly way. Nothing was too much for the people to do for us. And when we went on board ship to leave the island, they gave us everything we needed.
The Word of the Lord.

Gospel Acclamation
Alleluia, alleluia.
Jesus said:
"Don't stop the children coming to me."
Alleluia.

Gospel Mark 10:13, 14, 16
The reading comes from the Gospel of St. Mark. It is a story that surprised the friends of Jesus who, though tired, showed how much he liked to meet children.

People often used to bring children to Jesus and, when they did, Jesus always gave them his blessing. One day, however, some of the friends of Jesus told the children to go away. Jesus was angry when he saw this happening and he said: "Don't stop the children from coming to me. Don't send them away like that! Bring them back!" Then he put his arms around the children and he blessed them.
The Gospel of the Lord.

Prayer of the Faithful
God our Father, today we praise you for the lovely surprises you give us, all through the year. We thank you for eyes to see them, and for memories that hold them dear, making us always cheerful and happy.
1. Bless our parents, who think of our happiness, and plan nice surprises. Lord, hear us. R.
2. Bless our friends. May we treasure them for surprises, happiness, and fun together. Lord, hear us. R.
3. Bless the children in school. May they always be on the lookout, to give pleasant surprises in school, and at home. Lord, hear us. R.
4. Bless all of us here. May we use our gifts to bring surprises, pleasure and happiness to those we meet each day. Lord, hear us. R.
5. Bless everybody everywhere. May they always be aware of God's surprises, in the world around us. Lord, hear us. R.

Preparation of the Gifts
1. We bring a favorite toy. Our parents' love and goodness never cease to surprise us, too.
2. We bring a musical instrument. We use our gifts and talents, to give pleasure and surprises.
3. We bring a small seed. We are always amazed at God's surprises, and wonder at the beauty that can come from one tiny seed.

4. We bring our lives to God, with the bread and wine.

Second Prayer
God our Father, bless the gifts we give to you. May we share your gifts with others, because you have first given everything to us. We make this prayer through Jesus Christ, your Son, who lives and reigns with you in the unity of the Holy Spirit, one God forever and ever. Amen.

Communion Litany
RESPONSE: Lord, we thank you.

1. For springtime surprises, yellow flowers, and fresh green leaves. R.
2. For frisky young lambs, and soft yellow chicks. R.
3. For summer surprises, sunny skies, and golden sand. R.
4. For summer holidays, and long fun-filled days. R.
5. For autumn surprises, rich golden harvest, and red rosy apples. R.
6. For colorful, crackling, falling leaves. R.
7. For winter surprises, white snow silent around. R.
8. For the many surprises we give and receive. R.

Third Prayer
God our Father, you have given us Jesus himself. You have given us so many surprises of your love. Help us to surprise each other, and to make others happy. We make this prayer through Jesus Christ, your Son, who lives and reigns with you in the unity of the Holy Spirit, one God forever and ever. Amen.

Final Blessing
Go in peace, to live like Jesus, and to take note of all God's surprises.

32. The Sea

Today we're going to think about the sea—one of God's greatest and most powerful creations. Thinking about the sea should help us to see how great and how powerful God is.

First Prayer

God our Father, you have given us a wonderful world. Today we thank you especially for the sea which is so mighty and strong. Help us to understand how great you are. We ask this through Jesus, your Son, who lives and reigns with you, in the unity of the Holy Spirit, one God forever and ever. Amen.

First Reading Sirach 1:1,2,3,10

This reading comes from the book of a wise man called Sirach. God is wonderful—God understands everything. God has given us a wonderful world to live in —an exciting world—and there's so much to see in it.

God must be very wise.
God made every grain of sand on the beach
and there's so many of them
that we could never count them all.
God made every drop of rain that falls from the sky
and we couldn't count them all either.
Look up at the sky
and see how high it is above us!
Go up to the top of a high building
and look how far you can see
(and the land stretches away even further still!).
Go out on the sea in a boat
and look down into the water
and see how deep it is!
God is very, very wise,
and God wants all his friends

to become wise as God is wise.
The Word of the Lord.

Responsorial Psalm

RESPONSE: Lord God, how great you are.
1. How many are your works, Lord.
You have made them all because you are so wise. R.
2. The earth is full of your riches.
Everything you have made is wonderful. R.
3. There is the sea, vast and wide,
Full of moving things
past counting—
living things great and small. R.
4. The ships move in the sea,
And the monsters you made to play with.
Who will not praise you!
Who will not thank you! R.

Second Reading Psalm 106:23-30
This reading tells us about the mighty strength of God.

Sailors know the mighty strength of God.
They travel everywhere in ships
across the oceans of the world,
and they have seen the winds begin to blow
whipping up the water out at sea,
lifting up their ships high in the air
and dashing them back down into the depths.
Even sailors can become afraid
when they begin to stagger up on deck
like drunken men!
They know how to turn to God in danger.
God can change the storm to perfect stillness
and bring them safely home again to harbor.

The Word of the Lord.

Gospel Acclamation
Alleluia, alleluia,
Stand up, God and hear us.
Come and help us now.
Alleluia.

Gospel Mark 4:35-41
This reading comes from the Gospel of St. Mark. Water is strong and dangerous, that's why we must always be careful in the sea. It's very easy to drown. The reading tells the story of when the followers of Jesus thought they were going to be drowned in a storm at sea.

One night Jesus said to his friends,
"Let's go over to the other side of the lake."
So they left the big crowds
and got into a boat to go to the other side.
Then suddenly the wind began to blow,
and big waves splashed into the little boat
so that it started to fill with water.
But Jesus was so tired
he just lay down with his head on a cushion
and went to sleep.
His friends woke him up and said,
"Look! We're sinking.
Why aren't you doing something to help?"
So Jesus sat up
and he told the wind to stop making a noise,
and he told the waves to stop rocking the boat.
Suddenly the wind just died away
and the waves became calm again.
Then Jesus turned to his friends and said,
"Why are you so frightened?

You should have known by now
that I would not let you down."
The Gospel of the Lord.

Prayer of the Faithful
God our Father, you have given us a wonderful world. We thank you. Listen to our prayers:
1. The ever-rolling waves make us think of you, God, always loving us. Help us to keep on loving, too. Lord, hear us. R.
2. The big waves make us think of you, God, so mighty and strong. Help us to be strong and true to you in hard times. Lord, hear us. R.
3. The grains of sand make us think of you, God. Like you, they do not change or grow old. Help us to keep up the effort always. Lord, hear us. R.
5. The sky makes us think of you, God, who are everywhere. Help us to see you in the people and in the beauty everywhere around us. Lord, hear us. R.

Preparation of the Gifts
1. We bring sand, a gift from the sea.
2. We bring pebbles, a gift from the sea.
3. We bring shells, a gift from the sea.
4. We bring our lives to God, with the bread and wine.

Second Prayer
God our Father, we bring you our gifts of bread and wine. We bring you also the wonder and beauty of the great sea. We make our prayer through Jesus, your Son, who lives and reigns with you in the unity of the Holy Spirit, one God forever and ever. Amen.

Communion Litany
God our Father, what a wonderful world you have given us. We thank you for the wonders and pleasures of the sea.
RESPONSE: We thank you.
1. We thank you for pebbles, for rocks, and for cliffs. R.

1. We thank you for pebbles, for rocks, and for cliffs. R.
2. We thank you for sand dunes, for waves, and for the beach. R.
3. We thank you for fish, for shells, and for seaweed. R.
4. We thank you for the joys of the sea—for paddling, swimming, fishing, and boating. R.

Third Prayer

God our Father, you have given us Jesus in this holy meal. Help us to live like him, and help us to be your loving children. We ask this through Jesus, your Son, who lives and reigns with you in the unity of the Holy Spirit, one God forever and ever. Amen.

Final Blessing

Go in peace, to love God.

33. Trees

The theme of this Mass is trees. God has made the world beautiful with trees—trees of every shape and every size. Trees remind us of God's power, love and care. Today we praise God for God's love and care.

First Prayer

God our Father, trees show your power and love at work in the world. Help us to remember your love and care, when we see trees all around us. We ask this through Jesus, your Son, who lives and reigns with you in the unity of the Holy Spirit, one God forever and ever. Amen.

First Reading Psalm 1:3
Each year God cares for the trees. God cares for us too, looks after us, and protects us.

Down by the river is a good place for trees.
If the water flows near them, they never grow dry.
Their leaves are not withered, they stay green and alive.
And each year their branches are covered with fruit.
The man that is good is like a tree by the river.
God will look after him; God will protect him
and like a tree by the river he will grow strong.
The Word of the Lord.

Responsorial Psalm Psalm 49:10-11
Everything belongs to God. We praise God.
RESPONSE: Blessed be God.
1. Whenever you see the animals in the woods, they belong to me. R.
2. Whenever you see the cattle on the hillsides, remember who made them. R.
3. Whenever you see the birds up on the treetops, remember, I know each one of them. R.

---

4. Whenever you see a living thing out in the fields, think of me. R.

Second Reading Song of Songs 2:11-13
Trees change all the time. In springtime each year they grow new leaves. God looks after the trees at all times.

Whenever winter is finished, and the rain has stopped falling, then the plants begin to grow.
The birds sing and leaves appear on the trees and at last you can smell the perfume of the flowers. This is the time to sing for joy.
The Word of the Lord.

Gospel Acclamation
Alleluia, alleluia,
God said: "Let plants grow in the soil and let there be fruit trees."
Alleluia.

Gospel Mark 4:30-33
St. Mark tells us that God cares for the birds, too, and gives them the trees for their homes.

One day, Jesus said:
The mustard seed is the smallest seed in the world, but when you plant it in the ground it grows and becomes so big that the birds can come and build their nests in the shade of its branches.
Then Jesus said: God works like that.
The Gospel of the Lord.

Prayer of the Faithful
God our Father, we thank you for loving and caring for our families and our friends. We pray today for all those who help to make us happy.
1. We pray for those who cut wood in the forests and work in the lumber mills. Show them your love and care. Lord, hear us. R.

2. We pray for the builders, who use wood in our homes. Show them your love and care. Lord, hear us. R.

3. We pray for carpenters, who make furniture for our homes. Show them your love and care. Lord, hear us. R.

4. We pray for artisans, who make seats for our churches, and desks for our schools. Show them your love and care. Lord, hear us. R.

5. We pray for wood carvers, who carve wooden statues and other beautiful things. Show them your love and care. Lord, hear us. R.

Preparation of the Gifts

1. We bring a chair, made from wood.
2. We bring a guitar, made from wood.
3. We bring a carved statue, made from wood.
4. We bring our lives to God, with the bread and wine.

Second Prayer

God our Father, we bring you ourselves with our gifts of bread and wine. Through your power, love, and care, make our gifts and our lives into something great. We ask this through Jesus, your Son, who lives and reigns with you in the unity of the Holy Spirit, one God forever and ever. Amen.

Communion Litany

RESPONSE: Praise the Lord for trees.

1. For trees, with pale fresh green leaves in spring,
And for trees, with yellow, red, brown and gold leaves in autumn. R.

2. For trees, bare and leafless in winter,
And for living trees, hidden in coats of bark. R.

3. For trees with long, twisting branches,
And for trees that reach high in the sky. R.

4. For trees that are homes for birds and insects
And for trees that shelter animals from rain. R.

5. For trees that make wood for building homes
And for trees that make furniture for our homes. R.

Third Prayer

God our Father, Jesus your Son is close to us now. Help us to stay close to him, and to grow up to you like a tree—tall and strong. We ask this through Jesus, your Son, who lives and reigns with you in the unity of the Holy Spirit, one God forever and ever. Amen.

Final Blessing

Go in peace, to love God.

34. God Takes Care of Flowers

God must like flowers because God has filled our world with beautiful flowers of every color, shape, and size, and God takes good care of them all the time. If God takes such care of the flowers that soon die, God must surely take very good care of all of us, too.

First Prayer
God our Father, you have made this world beautiful with flowers of every color, and you take good care of them. Help us to know how much you care for us, too. We make this prayer through Jesus Christ, your Son, who lives and reigns with you in the unity of the Holy Spirit, one God forever and ever. Amen.

First Reading Isaiah 27:3, 4, 6
God likes flowers and God takes good care of them. God knows that they make the world beautiful, and that we like them too.

God says:
I am a gardener, and I look after my garden all day and all night. I keep watering all my plants because I don't want them to dry up or their leaves will fall off.

If I find any weeds I will pull them up. Then the whole of my garden will be filled with flowers.
The Word of the Lord.

Responsorial Psalm Psalm 1:3
We praise God the Father who gives us beautiful trees and flowers and takes care of them in summer and in winter.
RESPONSE: Give praise to God.
1. Down by the river is a good place for trees.
If the water flows near them, they will not grow dry. R.
2. Their leaves are not withered, they stay green and alive.
And each year their branches are covered with fruit. R.

3. The child that is good is like a tree by the river.
God will look after him. R.
4. God will protect him, and like a tree by the river he will grow strong. R.

Second Reading Song of Songs 2:11-13
Each year it is the same. Most flowers stop growing in winter but rise up again in spring to beautify the world.

When winter is finished, and the rain has stopped falling, then the plants begin to grow. The birds sing and leaves appear on the trees and at last you can smell the perfume of the flowers. This is the time to sing for joy!
The Word of the Lord.

Gospel Acclamation
Alleluia, alleluia.
If God takes so much trouble over the flowers
then God will certainly take good care of you.
Alleluia.

Gospel Luke 12:27-28
Jesus knew that God took good care of the flowers. He wanted people to know that God takes care of everything else as well, and especially of all of us.

One day, Jesus said:
Look at the flowers!
They don't worry about anything, and yet they look more beautiful than a king dressed in his best clothes! So don't worry about yourselves. If God takes so much care of the flowers then he will certainly take good care of you.
The Gospel of the Lord.

Prayer of the Faithful

God our Father, you watch over us and care for us. You care for us in dark days and in bright days. You care for us in winter and in summer. We thank you for your care of us all, and now we pray for our needs.

1. Bless our bishop and our priests who care for us in a special way. Lord, hear us. R.

2. Bless our parents whom you have given us to care for us. Lord, hear us. R.

3. Bless ourselves so that we will always make things easy for those who care for us. Lord, hear us. R.

4. Bless children everywhere and the people who care for them. Lord, hear us. R.

5. Bless the sick and those who care for them. Lord, hear us. R.

6. Bless the people who feel nobody cares about them. Lord, hear us. R.

Preparation of the Gifts

1. We bring flowers. Flowers are God's gift to us.

2. We bring water. God cares for the flowers and he cares for us too.

3. We bring our lives to God, with the bread and wine.

Second Prayer

God our Father, we bring you ourselves and our gift of flowers. May flowers ever bring us nearer to you. We make this prayer through Jesus Christ, your Son, who lives and reigns with you in the unity of the Holy Spirit, one God forever and ever. Amen.

Communion Litany

RESPONSE: We thank you, God.

1. For flowers that are red, blue, orange, and yellow, and for flowers that are white, golden, purple, and lilac. R.

2. For flowers that sway in the breeze, and for flowers that open in the sunlight. R.

3. For flowers that smell sweetly, and for flowers that make us joyful and happy. R.

4. For flowers that grow straight and tall, and for flowers that send out roots for food. R.

5. For flowers that are full of life and growing, and for flowers that speak to us of God. R.

Third Prayer

God our Father, we have come close to your Son, Jesus, in this holy communion. May the flowers, that speak to us of your goodness, ever help us to stay close to you. We make our prayer through Jesus Christ, your Son, who lives and reigns with you in the unity of the Holy Spirit, one God forever and ever. Amen.

Final Blessing

Go in peace, to love God.

35. The Holy Spirit

Today we are celebrating the coming of the Holy Spirit. One of the pictures God has given us to help us understand the Holy Spirit is wind. We will think about the wind as we try to understand the work of the Holy Spirit in our lives.

First Prayer
God our Father, we want to be like Jesus. Help us to listen to his Spirit when we pray. We ask this through Jesus, your Son, who lives and reigns with you in the unity of the Holy Spirit, one God forever and ever. Amen.

First Reading Acts 2:2-4
This reading comes from the story of the apostles. It tells us about the first time the Holy Spirit came to live in us.

The followers of Jesus were sitting together in one room,
when suddenly they heard the sound of a strong wind
blowing right through the whole house,
and they could see something
like flames of fire everywhere,
that came and touched each one of them.
In this way they were all filled with the Holy Spirit.
At once, they went outside
and began to tell everyone the story of Jesus.
There were people there
from every country in the world,
and they all heard the good news of Jesus!
The Word of the Lord.

Responsorial Psalm Psalm 103:1-4
God is so great, so important, you would hardly expect God to think about us at all, but God does.

RESPONSE: Glory to God.

1. Look up at the sun
and remember God is brighter still! R.

2. Look up at the sky
and remember it is nothing more than a little tent
in front of God! R.

3. The clouds that glide across the sky
are like chariots for God to ride in! R.

4. The rushing winds
merely blow against his face. R.

Second Reading Titus 3:4-7

This reading comes from one of the letters of St. Paul. It tells us that God our Father has given us the Holy Spirit as a special friend to help us.

Dear Titus,
When we were baptized, we all became the children of God.
This proves how good and kind God is,
because God still loved us
even though we did not deserve it!
When we were baptized, God gave us the spirit of God's love
to help us to be kind and loving as God is.
God did all this
because God wanted us to be his children
and to be happy with God for ever.
The Word of the Lord.

Gospel Acclamation

Alleluia, alleluia.
You will not be able to see me,
but you will have my Holy Spirit to help you and guide you.
Alleluia.

Gospel John 3:5-8

This reading comes from the gospel of St. John. It is part of the story of Ni-

codemus who came to see Jesus secretly, because he was afraid of what his friends might say if he came openly. The Holy Spirit was with him.

Jesus said to Nicodemus:
Only the Holy Spirit is strong enough
to help a man to live in God's way.
Strange things happen in our world.
Take the wind for example.
It blows where it wants to.
You can hear its noise,
but you haven't any idea
where it's coming from,
or where it's going to.
Doesn't that help you to understand
what the Holy Spirit is like
in the lives of people?
The Gospel of the Lord.

Prayer of the Faithful
God our Father, thank you for giving us your Holy Spirit to show us how to love. We pray that we may listen to the Holy Spirit guiding us all on our way to you.
1. Come, Holy Spirit, when our love and faith are tested by others making fun of us. Lord, hear us. R.
2. Come, Holy Spirit, when we have a hard job to do at home. Lord, hear us. R.
3. Come, Holy Spirit, to comfort the sick as we pray for them. Lord, hear us. R.
4. Come, Holy Spirit, when we try to give good example. Lord, hear us. R.
5. Come, Holy Spirit, when we care for someone who is sad or lonely. Lord, hear us. R.
6. Come, Holy Spirit, when we see that someone needs our help. Lord, hear us. R.

Preparation of the Gifts
1. We bring a lighted candle.
2. We bring our lives to God, with the bread and wine.

Second Prayer
God our Father, take our gifts and make them holy. Fill us with your Holy Spirit, who, like the wind, fills all of us with your power. We ask this through Jesus, your Son, who lives and reigns with you in the unity of the Holy Spirit, one God forever and ever. Amen.

Third Prayer
God our Father, make us generous, so that we can listen to your Spirit, and follow you with courage and love. We ask this through Jesus, your Son, who lives and reigns with you in the unity of the Holy Spirit, one God forever and ever. Amen.

Final Blessing
Go in peace, to love and serve God.

36. The Good Shepherd

Today we are thinking about Jesus, our good shepherd. He cares for us as a shepherd cares for his sheep. The good shepherd keeps the sheep from wandering or straying outside the fold. He leads the sheep to pasture, keeps them together, and protects them from danger.

First Prayer
God our Father, you have given us Jesus, our good shepherd, to love and care for us. Help us to be your loving children and to make our families happy. We ask this through Jesus, your Son, who lives and reigns with you in the unity of the Holy Spirit, one God forever and ever. Amen.

First Reading Ezekiel 34:3-6
This reading comes from the Book of Ezekiel. It is about shepherds taking good care of their sheep.

Shepherds should feed their sheep.
They should build them up if they are weak,
and take care of them when they are sick.
If any of the sheep get lost,
the shepherd should go after them,
in case they are left out on the cold mountainside
and the wild animals attack them and kill them.
If you are a good shepherd,
you must really look after your sheep.
The Word of the Lord.

Responsorial Psalm Psalm 100:1-3,5
RESPONSE: We are God's people and the sheep of God's pasture.
1. Make a joyful noise to the Lord, all the lands.
Serve the Lord with gladness. R.
2. Come before his presence with singing,
For the Lord is our God. R.

3. It is God who made us,
and not we ourselves.
We are God's people and the sheep of God's pasture. R.
4. For God is good,
God's mercy is everlasting. R.

Second Reading Micah 5:1-4
This reading comes from the Book of Micah. He tells us about Jesus who will look after us as a good shepherd looks after his sheep.

A long time ago
God spoke to the people of Bethlehem like this:
"I promise you,
the Great King will be born in Bethlehem.
He will look after you like a shepherd who looks after his sheep.
He will take care of you.
He will never let you down,
for he will be the King of the world!"
The Word of the Lord.

Gospel Acclamation
Alleluia, alleluia.
I am a shepherd and I'm a good shepherd.
I know all my sheep, every one of them, and they know me,
Alleluia.

Gospel John 10:3-5,14
This reading comes from the Gospel of St. John. Jesus is our good shepherd. He knows each one of us—he even knows our names. He is not a stranger to us, but is our friend, and we are glad to follow him.

One day, Jesus said:
Sheep listen to their own shepherd and they will follow him.
He can even call them one by one for he knows their names
and he can call them out of the sheepfold through the gate.

When they have all come out
he walks in front of them, and they will all follow
because they know the sound of his voice.
Of course, they would never follow a stranger
because they would not know the sound of his voice.
They would run away from him
if he told them to follow him.
Then Jesus said:
I am a shepherd and I'm a good shepherd
I know all my sheep, every one of them
and they know me.
The Gospel of the Lord.

Prayer of the Faithful

Lord, you are the good shepherd who never leaves your flock, You watch over us so that we feel safe in your love and care.

1. We pray for our mothers and fathers. Help them to look after their children like very good shepherds. Lord, hear us. R.

2. We pray for the shepherds of the church, our Pope, N., our Bishop, N., and all our priests. Help them to lead us all to your loving care. Lord, hear us. R.

3. We pray for all those who are preparing to be priests. Help them to keep on following your call. Lord, hear us. R.

4. We pray for ourselves. Help us to do what Jesus wants us to do. Lord, hear us. R.

5. We pray for all those who have died. Help them to be at peace in your loving presence. Lord, hear us. R.

Preparation of the Gifts

1. We bring a shepherd's crook.
2. We bring a shepherd's lantern.
3. We bring our lives to God, with the bread and wine.

Second Prayer

God our Father, accept our gifts and our whole selves. We place our-selves in your care, and in the care of Jesus, our good shepherd. Keep us all close to you. We ask this through Jesus, your Son, who lives and reigns with you in the unity of the Holy Spirit, one God forever and ever. Amen.

Third Prayer

God our Father, you have shared your love with us, by giving us Je-sus to care for us, like a good shepherd. May we always follow him. We ask this through Jesus, your Son, who lives and reigns with you in the unity of the Holy Spirit, one God forever and ever. Amen.

Final Blessing

Go in peace, to love God.

37. Mary, Mother of Jesus

The theme is Mary, Mother of Jesus. Mary prepared for the coming of Jesus in a very special way. When God chose her to be the mother of Jesus, she said "Yes" to God, that she would be the mother of Jesus. Mary always said "Yes" to God.

First Prayer
God our Father, we have come together to thank you for Mary, Mother of Jesus, and our mother, too. She always did what you wanted her to do. Help us to listen to you, and to do what you want with joy. We make our prayer through Jesus, your Son, who lives and reigns with you in the unity of the Holy Spirit, one God forever and ever. Amen.

First Reading Isaiah 41:9-10
Isaiah tells us that God chooses every one of us to do a special job in life. But whatever God wants us to do, God promises to help us to do it well.

God says:
"I have chosen you.
You are working for me now.
So do not be afraid.
I am with you—don't worry!
I am your God, and I will make you strong.
You can hold my hand and I will help you."
The Word of the Lord.

Responsorial Psalm Luke 1:46-55
This is Mary's song of love, praise and thanks to God. She was full of joy and happiness.
RESPONSE: God has been good to me.
1. Mary said, "My heart sings with thanks.
God is great and good.

Holy is God's name." R.
2. "God has smiled on me.
God looks kindly on all poor people.
Holy is God's name." R.
3. "God is mighty and powerful.
God has done great things for me.
Holy is God's name." R.
4. "God remembers his people.
God has done marvelous deeds for me.
Holy is God's name." R.

Second Reading Isaiah 12:4-6
God our Father is wonderful. With Mary, we would like to tell the whole wide world how good God is!

I want to tell the whole wide world
—God has been good to me.
I want to tell the whole wide world
—God is wonderful.
I want to sing and to shout, because I am happy.
For God has come to me, and God is great.
The Word of the Lord.

Gospel Acclamation
Alleluia, alleluia,
Rejoice, Mary, for the Lord has blessed you,
and God is with you, now!
Alleluia.

Gospel Luke 1:26-31, 38
When God chose Mary to be the Mother of Jesus she said, "Yes. I'll do anything you want!"'

One day, God sent his messenger to a town called Nazareth, to a girl called Mary who was engaged to a man called Joseph.

The messenger said, "Rejoice, Mary, for the Lord has blessed you, and God is with you now!"

Mary didn't know what to say and she wondered what this meant. But the messenger said: "Do not be afraid—God is very pleased with you.

"Listen, you are going to have a baby, and you will call him Jesus."

Then Mary said: "I am the servant of God. I am glad to do whatever God wants."

The Gospel of the Lord.

Prayer of the Faithful

God our Father, we ask you now to bless us, and to help us always to do what you want us to do.

1. We pray for our Pope, our bishop and our priests. Help them to do what God wants them to do. Lord, hear us. R.

2. We pray for our parents, our brothers and our sisters. Help them to do what God wants them to do. Lord, hear us. R.

3. We pray for our teachers, and all our friends at school. Help them to do what God wants them to do. Lord, hear us. R.

4. We pray for the people who work for us. Help them to do what God wants them to do. Lord, hear us. R.

5. We pray for ourselves, and for children everywhere. Help them to do what God wants them to do. Lord, hear us. R.

Preparation of the Gifts

1. We bring a statue of Mary. Mary did what God wanted her to do.

2. We bring a Bible. Mary listened and said "Yes" to God.

3. We bring a rose. We show our love for Mary.

4. We bring our lives to God, with the bread and wine.

Second Prayer

God our Father, we bring our gifts and ourselves to you. Take us and bless us and help us to do always what you want us to do. We make our prayer through Jesus, your Son, who lives and reigns with you in the unity of the Holy Spirit, one God forever and ever. Amen.

Communion Litany

RESPONSE: Thank you, God, for Mary.

1. Mary was the Mother of Jesus at Bethlehem. R.
2. Mary loved and cared for Jesus. R.
3. Mary brought Jesus to the Temple for the Presentation. R.
4. Mary brought Jesus on pilgrimage to Jerusalem. R.
5. Mary saw Jesus leave home to tell the Good News. R.
6. Mary was with Jesus as he died on the cross. R.
7. Mary saw Jesus after he rose from the dead. R.
8. Mary was with the apostles when the Holy Spirit came to them. R.

Third Prayer

God our Father, Jesus has come to us in this holy communion. Help us to stay close to him, as we try to do what you want us to do. We make this prayer through Jesus, your Son, who lives and reigns with you in the unity of the Holy Spirit, one God forever and ever. Amen.

Final Blessing

Go in peace, to do what God wants you to do.

38. St. Paul: Explorer and Traveler

Today we remember St. Paul. God had special work for him to do. He had to tell the Good News everywhere—across the sea and far from home—the Good News of God's loving care for everybody.

First Prayer
God our Father, you chose Paul to bring the Good News to others. Help us to be Good News to others, by the way we live. We make this prayer through Jesus Christ, your Son, who lives and reigns with you in the unity of the Holy Spirit, one God forever and ever. Amen.

First Reading Romans 15:17-20
In this reading we hear about Paul's one ambition of telling the story of Jesus where his name had not been heard.
Dear friends,
I'm proud of what I've been able to do to make God's way known throughout the world. But it's only through Jesus I've been able to do what I have done. There is one thing—and one thing only—I care to talk about: how Jesus has used me to help people of many lands to love in God's way.

From Jerusalem in Palestine, all around the world, I have made the Good News of Jesus sound like the Good News it is—Good News for everybody. For I have had one ambition: to tell the story of Jesus where his name has not been heard.
The Word of the Lord.

Responsorial Psalm Isaiah 43:10
This hymn of praise tells of the mission of Jesus who was sent by God to bring the Good News to all.
RESPONSE: God sent me to bring the Good News to the poor.

1. You yourselves are my witnesses—it is the Lord who speaks—the

people whom I have chosen. R.

2. The Spirit of the Lord has been given to me. God has made me holy. R.

3. God has sent me to bring Good News to the poor. He has sent me to make broken hearts happy again. R.

Gospel Acclamation
Alleluia, alleluia.
Jesus said,
"I want you to go everywhere and tell everyone what I have done."
Alleluia.

Gospel Acts 1:6-14
Jesus wants everyone to come to him, then they will get to know and love the Father and receive the Holy Spirit.

Jesus and his friends were together on a hill in Galilee. Jesus said to them: You will be given God's own power when his spirit comes into your hearts. Then your business will be to go all over the world and tell everybody what you know about me. You must start here in this city first of all, go out into your own homeland, and then right to the very ends of the earth.
The Word of the Lord.

Prayer of the Faithful
God our Father, we pray for your children in this place, our brothers and sisters in other places, and all over the world.

1. Lord, help us to spread the Good News, by the things we say and do for others. Lord, hear us. R.

2. Lord, help us to spread the Good News, by being friend and neighbor to all. Lord, hear us. R.

3. Lord, help us to spread the Good News, by sharing and enjoying the good things of God's beautiful world. Lord, hear us. R.

4. Lord, help us to spread the Good News, by being loving, gener-

ous, and understanding. Lord, hear us. R.

5. Lord, help us to spread the Good News, by letting others know they are important to us. Lord, hear us. R.

Preparation of the Gifts

1. We bring a newspaper and a radio. We read for ourselves, and we listen to the news of the world.

2. We bring a Bible—the Word of God. We read the Bible, and we listen to God speaking to us.

3. We bring our lives to God, with the bread and wine. We bring our words and deeds, the things we say and do, to spread the Good News.

Second Prayer

God our Father, we bring these gifts to you, signs of our love. Accept them, with our effort to spread the Good News. We make this prayer through Jesus Christ, your Son, who lives and reigns with you in the unity of the Holy Spirit, one God forever and ever. Amen.

Third Prayer

God our Father, Jesus is with us in holy communion. May he help us to be untiring, like Paul, in our work of spreading the Good News. We make this prayer through Jesus Christ, your Son, who lives and reigns with you in the unity of the Holy Spirit, one God forever and ever. Amen.

Final Blessing

Go in peace, and spread the Good News wherever you are.

39. St. Patrick

Today we are thinking about St. Patrick, the patron saint of Ireland. St. Patrick spent his life trying to love God. We ask him today to come and be with us, to help us grow in God's love.

First Prayer
God our Father, you chose St. Patrick to bring the Good News to the people of Ireland. Help us to bring the love of Jesus to others, just as Patrick did. We ask this through Jesus, you Son, who lives and reigns with you in the unity of the Holy Spirit, one God forever and ever. Amen.

First Reading Psalm 112
This is an Old Testament reading that tells us that people who do good will never be forgotten.

Happy are those who never did wrong,
and who did not want gold or riches.
They are the ones
whose lives we admire.
They could have been bad,
but they were not bad.
They could have done wrong,
but they did no wrong.
The good things they did
will never be forgotten.
The whole church will speak of how kind
and generous they were.
The Word of the Lord.

Responsorial Psalm Psalm 130:2-3
Again and again the Book of Psalms says "You can always trust God."
RESPONSE: I trust in God.

1. I saw a mother
carrying her baby in her arms
so gently,
so quietly. R.
2. I am at peace,
like that baby,
and I am happy.
I trust in God. R.

Second Reading Galatians 1:15-16
This reading is from one of St. Paul's letters.

God had marked me out for my great work
before I was born, and now, in God's love,
God has called me to do it.
God has shown me God's son;
and my business now is
to tell the story of Jesus to everybody,
all over the world.
I owe everything I am
To God's love.
The Word of the Lord.

Gospel Acclamation
Alleluia, alleluia.
You did not choose me.
Remember, I chose you,
Alleluia.

Gospel John 15;15-16
The gospel reading comes from the Gospel of St. John.
Jesus said to his apostles:
"I don't want you to be my 'slaves,'
just doing the things you are told to do,

without knowing at all why you are doing them.
I want you to be my 'friends':
that's why I have shared with you
all that I have learned from my Father.
You did not choose me, you remember,
I chose you."
The Gospel of the Lord.

Prayer of the Faithful
God our Father, you sent St. Patrick to preach your love to the people of Ireland. Help us to grow in your love by following his example.
1. May St. Patrick help us to be faithful to Christ and his teaching. Lord, hear us. R.
2. May St. Patrick help us to bring the goodness of God to all we meet. Lord, hear us. R.
3. May St. Patrick help us to bring love and peace to our country. Lord, hear us. R.
4. May St. Patrick help Irish missionaries in foreign countries. Lord, hear us. R.
5. May St. Patrick help to make our homes places of prayer. Lord, hear us. R. 6. May St. Patrick help those who leave home to look for work. Lord, hear us. R.

Let us say together St Patrick's favorite prayer:
Christ be with me
Christ be beside me
Christ be before me
Christ be behind me
Christ be at my right hand
Christ be at my left hand
Christ be with me everywhere I go
Christ be my friend forever and ever. Amen.

Preparation of the Gifts

God chose St. Patrick to bring God's message of love to the Irish people. Now we bring to God our tokens of love.

1. We bring the shamrock.
2. We bring a missal.
3. We bring rosary beads.
4. We bring our lives to God, with the bread and wine.

Second Prayer

God our Father, we bring you our whole lives with these gifts of bread and wine. Help us as we remember the love of St. Patrick, to live in peace, and love each other more. We ask this through Jesus, your Son, who lives and reigns with you in the unity of the Holy Spirit, one God forever and ever. Amen.

Third Prayer

God our Father, you have brought us together in the love of Jesus. Help us. like St. Patrick, to go on bringing the love of Jesus to others. We ask this through Jesus your Son, who lives and reigns with you in the unity of the Holy Spirit, one God forever and ever. Amen.

Final Blessing

Go in peace, to love God.

40. Advent

In this Advent theme we think about our response to God's call to love. We apologize to God for the times we say "no." During Advent we make an effort to say "yes" to God and to follow God's way of love.

First Prayer
God our Father, help us during this time of Advent to be your friends. Help us to see the wrong in our lives and make us ready to follow your way of love. We make this prayer through Jesus, your Son, who lives and reigns with you in the unity of the Holy Spirit, one God forever and ever. Amen.

First Reading Isaiah 9: 1-2, 6-7
Isaiah tells us that Jesus is like a bright light. His light lights up the path we must walk on our way to God the Father.

Once upon a time, everyone lived in the dark but now—we can see!
They used to live in a world that was full of shadows but now—we have a light to light up our way!
We have God with us and God has made us happy.
God has sent us a child who is to be our King, and he will keep everyone safe.
The Word of the Lord.

Responsorial Psalm Ps 10
If we stay close to God our Father, we will be safe and secure.
RESPONSE: God our Father, we will stay close to you.
1. I won't fly away when people attack me.
I trust in the Lord and I will be safe. R.
2. I know God can see me—God can see everybody.
God knows who is good and who is bad. R.
3. Because God is so good, God loves to see goodness.
God hates to see violence. R.

---

4. So we can be sure that, if we do what is right,
we can live close beside God, safe and secure. R.

Second Reading Ephesians 1:3-6

St. Paul tells us that God our Father loves us in the same way that God loves Jesus, because we also are God's children! That's why we say "thank you" to God.

Dear friends,
Give thanks to God the Father
who has made us brothers of Christ!
Even before the world was made,
God chose us to be God's very own people
—the People of Christ.
God wanted us to live as God does in goodness and friendship,
for God had decided that we should be God's own children.
God loved us so much that God wanted us to be God's sons and daughters.
Let us praise God.
The Word of the Lord.

Gospel Acclamation

Alleluia, alleluia,
Someone is coming after me and he is much more important than I am.
Alleluia.

Gospel Luke 3: 10-11, 14-16

In this reading St. Luke tells us that John the Baptist prepared the way for Jesus. He told the people what they should do to change their lives and to follow the way of the Lord.

Lots of people came to John the Baptist and said: "What do we have to do?" John said: "Share things with each other, and don't be

greedy, either!" Everyone thought John was going to be the great king, and they all began to get excited. But John said: "I am not the great king that God promised to send. Someone else is coming after me, and he is much more important than I am. "In fact, he is so great that I am not even good enough to untie his shoe-laces!"
The Gospel of the Lord.

Prayer of the Faithful

God our Father, we come to you today with all our needs and the needs of all our friends.

1. Bless our Holy Father, the Pope, our bishops, and our priests. Help them to follow your way. Lord, hear us. R.

2. Bless all our friends. Help them to follow your way. Lord, hear us. R.

3. Bless our teachers and all who work for us. Help them to follow your way. Lord, hear us. R.

4. Bless all of us, your children. Help us to follow your way. Lord, hear us. R.

5. Bless all our friends at home and away. Help them to follow your way. Lord, hear us. R.

Preparation of the Gifts

1. We bring a lighted candle (or Advent wreath). Jesus is the light that lights up our way.

2. We bring a Bible. Jesus is the way to the Father.

3. We bring our lives to God, with the bread and wine.

Second Prayer

God our Father, we bring you our gifts of bread and wine and we bring ourselves with our gifts. Bless our gifts and bless us, too. We make our prayer through Jesus, your Son, who lives and reigns with you in the unity of the Holy Spirit, one God forever and ever. Amen.

Third Prayer

God our Father, you have given us your Son, Jesus. Help us to stay close to him always and to follow his way of love. We make this prayer through Jesus, your Son, who lives and reigns with you in the unity of the Holy Spirit, one God forever and ever. Amen.

Final Blessing

Go in peace, to love God.

41. Christmas

Today is Christmas Day—a day of joy. The birth of Jesus brought joy to the world. It brought joy to Mary and Joseph, the shepherds, and the wise men. Today we share their joy.

First Prayer
God our Father, you sent your Son, Jesus, to show us your love, and to help us to love. Help us to listen to him and to do what you want us to do. We make our prayer through Jesus, your Son, who lives and reigns with you in the unity of the Holy Spirit, one God forever and ever. Amen.

First Reading Isaiah 60: 1, 26, 29
Isaiah tells us in this reading that Jesus is like the sun that fills the world with daylight. He filled the world with happiness, goodness, and joy.
In the beginning, the world was filled with darkness, and it was as black as night. But God came and changed all that! God filled the world with God's light instead, just like the sun that shines in the sky every morning.
The Word of the Lord.

Responsorial Psalm Psalm 17: 2, 4, 29
This is a song of praise, joy, and thanks because God has been so good to us.
RESPONSE: God has been good to us.
1. I love you, my Lord,
for you have made me strong. R.
2. I thank you, my Lord, for you have heard my prayer. R.
3. You have been like a light before my eyes.
You have made my darkness into light. R.
4. I thank you, my Lord, for you have heard my prayer. R.

Second Reading Galatians 4:4-6

St. Paul tells us that Jesus came to help us all. He came to give us the chance to be God's children and part of God's family.

Dear friends,

When the right time came, God the Father sent Jesus to us.

Jesus had a mother just like the rest of us and he had to do as he was told—like us. He wanted to help us all, and he came to give us the chance to become like "children of God," so that we could call God "Our Father"—like him.

The Word of the Lord.

Gospel Acclamation

Alleluia, alleluia,

Glory to God in the highest

and peace to God's people on earth.

Alleluia.

Gospel Luke 2:4-7

This is the story of the birth of Jesus in Bethlehem.

Joseph lived in the town of Nazareth, but one day he had to go all the way to Bethlehem with Mary, even though she was going to have a baby. While they were in Bethlehem, the baby was born—it was Mary's first child, and she dressed him up in baby clothes and made a bed for him in a stable because there was no room left for them at the inn.

The Gospel of the Lord.

Prayer of the Faithful

God our Father, Jesus came to show your love to all people. We ask you now to help us to share this love for all who are poor and in need, at this time.

1. We pray for people who are sleeping outside this Christmas, because they have no homes to live in. Lord, help us to share your love. Lord, hear us. R.

2. We pray for people who are hungry this Christmas, because they have no food to eat. Lord, help us to share your love. Lord, hear us. R.

3. We pray for people who are cold this Christmas, because they have no warm clothes, or fuel. Lord, help us to share your love. Lord, hear us. R.

4. We pray for the sick and the old this Christmas, because they have nobody to care for them. Lord, help us to share your love. Lord, hear us. R.

5. We pray for people who are lonely and alone this Christmas, because they are forgotten by everyone. Lord, help us to share your love. Lord, hear us. R.

6. We pray for people who are sad this Christmas, because their friends have gone away or have died. Lord, help us to share your love. Lord, hear us. R.

Preparation of the Gifts
1. We bring a candle. Jesus, our Light, has come.
2. We bring a crown. Jesus, Prince of Peace, has come.
3. We bring a crucifix. Jesus, our Friend, has come.
4. We bring our lives to God, with the bread and wine.

Second Prayer
God our Father, we bring our gifts of bread and wine. With these gifts we bring our lives. Take our gifts in the name of Christ, your Son, who lives and reigns with you in the unity of the Holy Spirit, one God forever and ever. Amen.

Third Prayer
God our Father, we have come close to Jesus in this communion. Help us to love one another and to make our world a happy, joyful, and loving place. We make our prayer through Jesus Christ, your

Son, who lives and reigns with you in the unity of the Holy Spirit, one God forever and ever. Amen.

Final Blessing
Go in peace, to love God.

42. Winter

Today we are thinking about winter. There are many things about winter that we do not like, especially the weather. Everything seems to be dead, but this is not so. Winter is only a time of waiting for the new life of spring.

First Prayer
God our Father, even in winter you care for the trees, the flowers, the seeds, and all living things. Help us to know your love and care for us at all times, too. We ask this through Jesus, your Son, who lives and reigns with you in the unity of the Holy Spirit, one God forever and ever. Amen.

First Reading Psalm 147
This reading comes from Psalm 147. It is a song about winter.
Praise God:
He gives an order.
His word flashes to earth.
The snow falls down as thick as cotton wool—because God says so!
God scatters frost upon the earth—like talcum powder!
God fires hailstones from the sky—like breadcrumbs!
Then, just as suddenly,
God sends the winds to blow away the ice
and melt the rivers!
The word of the Lord.

Responsorial Psalm Psalm 99:1-5
In this poem we say "thank you" to God, because we know God is interested in us and cares for us.
RESPONSE: We thank you, Lord, we praise you, Lord, for you are good and loving.
1. Let everyone be happy,
let everyone be glad,
let everyone be full of joy

and sing to the Lord our God. R.
2. We know the Lord is God
God gives us life and breath,
For we are God's own family
And we belong to God. R.

Second Reading Song of Songs 2:11-13

This reading is from the Song of Songs. During the winter the flowers stop growing. But we can look forward to spring when they come up once more. This happens every year.

When winter is finished,
and the rain has stopped falling,
then the plants begin to grow.
The birds sing
and leaves appear on the trees,
and at last you can smell the perfume of the flowers.
This is the time to sing for joy!
The Word of the Lord.

Third Reading Romans 8:28,29

This reading comes from one of the letters of St. Paul. God our Father gives all of us a job to do.

Dear friends,
God is making things better all the time.
God knows all the people who love him,
and gives them each a job to do,
so they can work with God.
God wants us all to become more like Jesus,
for Jesus is our eldest brother
in the family of God.
The Word of the Lord.

Gospel Acclamation
Alleluia, alleluia.
Soon the winter will be over and gone.
Alleluia.

Gospel Mark 13:28
This reading comes from St. Mark's Gospel.

Jesus says:
The fig tree can teach us something.
Its branch is leafless in the winter.
When it begins to bud and the leaves come out,
summer is here.
The Gospel of the Lord.

Prayer of the Faithful
God our Father, we thank you for all the blessings of winter. Plant your own life and love deep in us and in those for whom we pray.
1. We pray for our mothers and fathers, who take good care of our lives. Lord, hear us. R.
2. We pray for all in our school who look after our needs. Lord, hear us. R.
3. We pray for farmers, and for all those who work to provide food for us. Lord, hear us. R.
4. We pray for the doctors and nurses, who care for us when we are ill. Lord, hear us. R.
5. We pray for our sick friends, and for our friends who have died. Lord, hear us. R.

Preparation of the Gifts
1. We bring a loaf of bread and a cup of broth. We need nourishing food in winter.
2. We bring a warm sweater and a pair of gloves. We need warm clothes in winter.

3. We bring a hot water bottle and some cough medicine. We need medical care in winter.

4. We bring our lives to God, with the bread and wine.

Second Prayer

God our Father, we bring you our gifts. Help us to remember your gifts to us, especially those you give us in winter. We ask this through Jesus, your Son, who lives and reigns with you, in the unity of the Holy Spirit, one God forever and ever. Amen.

Third Prayer

God our Father, you have given us your Son, Jesus, in this Mass. May we go out now to help, to care, and to share like him. We ask this through Jesus, your Son, who lives and reigns with you in the unity of the Holy Spirit, one God forever and ever. Amen.

Final Blessing

Go in peace, to love God.

43. New Life in Spring

Today we are going to think about the new life of spring and about the new and everlasting life of Jesus, from the first Easter Day.

First Prayer
God our Father, in springtime you wake up the whole world to new life. We see life in flowers and trees, in birds and in animals. May this new life help us to know you better. We ask this through Jesus, your son, who lives and reigns with you in the unity of the Holy Spirit, one God forever and ever. Amen.

First Reading
This reading is a poem called Spring Prayer, *by Ralph Waldo Emerson.*

For flowers that bloom about our feet,
for tender grass, so fresh, so sweet,
For song of bird, and hum of bee,
For all things fair, we hear, or see,
Father, in heaven, we thank Thee.
For blue of stream, and blue of sky
For pleasant shade, of branches high,
For fragrant air, and cooling breeze,
For beauty of the blooming trees,
Father in Heaven, we thank Thee.

Responsorial Psalm Psalm 64:10-14
God our Father makes this world of ours alive. That's why we give God thanks.
RESPONSE: God is great! Sing for joy!
1. You are the one who sends down early rain,
to prepare the soil for the seeds. R.
2. You are the one who gathers rain into the rivers,
to carry water to the crops. R.

3. You are the one who gives us gentle showers,
to soak into the hard ploughed fields to soften the earth and make
the plants sprout and grow. R.
4. You are the one who gives us the harvest,
filling the valley with golden wheat,
and fattening the sheep on the green hillsides. R.
5. Let everyone give thanks to you for all your blessings,
and sing for joy. R.

Second Reading Song of Songs 2:11,12,13
The second reading is from the Song of Songs. During the winter most of the
flowers stop growing, but in spring they rise up again.

When winter is finished,
and the rain has stopped falling,
then the plants begin to grow.
The birds sing
and leaves appear on the trees
and at last you can smell the perfume of the flowers.
This is the time to sing for joy!
The Word of the Lord.

Third Reading 1 Corinthians 15:3-8
This reading is from one of the letters of St. Paul. A lot of people saw Jesus
after he had been raised to life again. That's one way we know that he is still
alive now.

Dear friends,
Jesus died, and he was buried,
but God the Father raised him up to life again.
After this, many people saw Jesus.
First, Peter saw him, next, "the Twelve,"
then, five hundred people all at the same time!
Then James, and all the others.

And last of all, I saw him as well.
The Word of the Lord.

Gospel Acclamation
Alleluia, alleluia.
See, winter is past.
The rains are over and gone.
The flowers appear on the earth.
The season of glad songs has come.
The song of birds is heard in our land.
Alleluia.

Gospel John 20:26-29
This reading is from the Gospel of St. John.

One week later, Jesus came to them all a second time, and he said to Thomas, "Look! here are my hands, hold them! Feel the wound in my side as well!" And Thomas said, "You are my Lord and my God!" Then Jesus said, "You know that I am alive because you can see me. May God bless all those people who will not be able to see me but will still believe in me!
The Gospel of the Lord.

Prayers of the Faithful
God our Father, you have given us everything good and beautiful, especially in the springtime. Listen to us as we pray.
1. We believe that Jesus rose to new and better life.
Help us to live a new and better life. Lord, hear us. R.
2. Help all of us to show real love to each other. Lord, hear us. R.
3. Help all of us to live as your brothers and sisters. Lord, hear us. R.
4. Help all of us to be kind to those who have no friends. Lord, hear us. R.
5. Help all of us to say thanks for the good things you give us. Lord, hear us. R.

Preparation of the Gifts

1. We bring buds, signs of new life.
2. We bring spring flowers, signs of new life.
3. We bring a picture of a mother and baby.
4. We bring our lives to God, with the bread and wine.

Second Prayer

God our Father, here are our gifts of bread and wine. With them, we bring you the new life of spring. We make this prayer through our Lord Jesus, your Son, who lives and reigns with you in the unity of the Holy Spirit, one God forever and ever. Amen.

Communion Litany

RESPONSE: Thank you, God.

1. Thank you, God, for this lovely time of year; for flowers full of life and color. R.
2. Thank you, God, for new life everywhere around; for growing seeds, full of life and movement. R.
3. Thank you, God, for birds full of life, bursting out of shells, hungry, growing, and then flying. R.
4. Thank you, God, for babies full of life, loving their mothers, and able to enjoy play. R.
5. Thank you, God, for children full of life, running, skipping and laughing. R. 6. Thank you, God, for parents, working, consoling, and helping. R.
7. Thank you, God, for Jesus, full of life, sharing his new life with us. R.

Third Prayer

God our Father, you have given us Jesus, your Son, in holy communion. May we share his love with others. We ask this through Jesus, your Son, who lives and reigns with you in the unity of the Holy Spirit, one God forever and ever. Amen.

Final Blessing
Go in peace, to love God.

44. Lent

Today we are thinking about Lent and about doing difficult things. During Lent we try to do without something we like, or pray a bit more often. We try to do without things, so that we can give more of what we have to others.

First Prayer

God our Father, during Lent you ask us to give up things we enjoy and to be more generous toward others. Help us to do this cheerfully for the whole of Lent. We ask this through Jesus, your Son, who lives and reigns with you in the unity of the Holy Spirit, one God forever and ever. Amen.

First Reading

This is the story of Fr. Damian who did something difficult for God.

There was once a boy called Damian who became a priest when he grew up. He heard of a faraway island called Molokai, where lepers lived. He left his family and friends and set sail for Molokai. He arrived there weeks later. What he saw made him very sad. The people suffered so much pain that they were always fighting among themselves. After a short time on the island, he got on another ship and sailed home.

He needed medicine and bandages for the lepers. When he had collected enough, he set sail for Molokai again. His own people didn't want him to go back, but he was doing God's work, and nothing would stop him. He arrived back in Molokai after weeks and weeks on the ship.

He showed the people how to build houses, sow gardens, and grow vegetables. They got together and built a hospital. Fr Damian taught them how to live together and love each other. He did something big for God.

Responsorial Psalm Psalm 112

RESPONSE: What we do for each other, we do for God.

1. Happy the children who do
what the Lord wants them to do. R.
2. God's children
will be rewarded
for their goodness. R.
3. God's children
will be rich
and happy forever. R.

Second Reading 2 Corinthians 11:23.25-27

This reading is from one of the letters of St. Paul where he wrote about the hard things he had to do to follow in the footsteps of Jesus.

Dear friends,
These are some of the things that have happened to me while I have
been telling people about Jesus.
I have had to work very hard.
I've been sent to prison.
I've been beaten up (in fact, I was nearly killed once).
I've been shipwrecked (and once I was lost out at sea all night!).
I've always been on the move
and I've often been afraid
that I was going to be attacked by bandits.
I've had to get across rivers
when there's been no bridge to walk over.
I've often had to go on working
without going to bed all night.
Sometimes I've been so hungry and thirsty
that I've nearly died!
Once I even had some soldiers chasing me
and I had to get away by hiding in a basket
and my friends lowered me out of their window

over the city walls
so that I could escape and go free.
Nevertheless, I can put up with all this
because I am doing it all for the sake of Jesus.
The Word of the Lord.

Gospel Acclamation
Alleluia, alleluia.
When we do something for each other,
we do it for God.
Alleluia.

Gospel Matthew 35:34-36
The gospel reading comes from the Gospel of St. Matthew.

Jesus said to his friends:
"On the last day I will say –
'I was hungry and you gave me food;
I was thirsty and you gave me drink;
I was a foreigner and you took me home with you;
I was in rags and you gave me clothes;
I fell ill and you looked after me;
I was in prison and you came to see me.
Believe me—
When you helped the least of my brothers,
you helped me.'"
The Gospel of the Lord.

Prayer of the Faithful
God our Father, you sent your son, Jesus, to show us how much you care for us and for our happiness. In our concern for the happiness of others, we pray:
1. For those who haven't got enough—that we may be generous toward them this Lent. Lord, hear us. R,

2. For mothers and fathers—that they may give their children the care they need. Lord, hear us. R.

3. For our teachers and friends—that we may all work together to make the classroom a happy place. Lord, hear us. R.

4. For the sick and the suffering—that they may soon be well again. Lord, hear us. R.

5. For the old and the lonely—that someone may care. Lord, hear us. R.

6. For those who have died—that they may live with you forever. Lord, hear us. R.

Preparation of the Gifts

1. We bring a crucifix—Jesus died for us all.

2. We bring a mission box—we do without so that we can give to others.

3. We bring a loaf of bread—our savings help to feed the hungry.

4. We bring our lives to God, with the bread and wine.

Second Prayer

God our Father, we offer our whole lives as we give you our gifts of bread and wine. We also bring you our Lenten efforts. Let us grow in your love by sharing and by doing good things. We ask this through Jesus, your Son, who lives and reigns with you in the unity of the Holy Spirit, one God forever and ever. Amen.

Third Prayer

God our Father, we have shared your life and love by meeting Jesus in this Mass. Help us to go out and share this life and love with everybody we meet today. We make our prayer through Jesus, your Son, who lives and reigns with you in the unity of the Holy Spirit, one God forever and ever. Amen.

Final Blessing

Go in peace, to love God.

45. Palm Sunday

Today, Palm Sunday, is the beginning of Holy Week. In today's Mass, we think of Christ's joyful journey into his own city, Jerusalem, where he was to suffer, to die, and to rise again.

Blessing of Palms
Let us pray.
God our Father, bless these branches and make them holy. Today we joyfully praise Jesus, our king. May we one day come to the happiness of heaven, by following Jesus, who lives and reigns for ever and ever. Amen.

Gospel Matthew 21:1-3,6-9
This is a reading from St Matthew's Gospel.

When they arrived at the Olive Hill,
Jesus said to two of his friends.
"If you go into that village over there,
you will find a donkey and its foal, just as you go in.
Untie them and bring them here.
If anyone asks you who they are for,
tell them they're for me,
and I will send them back as soon as I can."
So off they went
and they brought back the donkey and foal
with their coats spread over the animals' backs,
and Jesus then got on.
Some people even put their coats on the ground
in front of Jesus.
Others cut branches off the trees
and put them on the ground for Jesus to ride over.
There were lots of people,
walking in front of Jesus

and walking behind him,
and they all shouted
"Hosanna, Hosanna!
Blessed is he who comes
in the name of the Lord!
Hosanna, Hosanna!"
The Gospel of the Lord.

The Procession Begins
Let us go in peace
praising Jesus our king,
like the crowds who welcomed him to Jerusalem.

First Prayer
God our Father, we love you, our Lord and king. Help us to be loving children of your kingdom, now and always. We ask this through Jesus, your Son, who lives and reigns with you in the unity of the Holy Spirit, one God forever and ever. Amen.

First Reading Zechariah 9:9
This reading is from the Book of Zechariah.

Everyone shouts, "Here is the King!"
Everyone is happy, for he is strong,
and gentle as well,
for he rides on a donkey and her foal!
The Word of the Lord.

Responsorial Psalm Psalm 24:7-10
RESPONSE: Glory and praise to you, God our king.
1. Glory and praise to you,
God our king. R.
2. Open the gates!
Open the doors!
The King of Glory

wants to come in. R.
3. Who is the King of Glory?
He is the Lord,
strong and mighty. R.
4. Open the gates,
open the doors of your hearts,
so that the King may come in. R.
5. Who is the King of Glory?
He is the Lord, our God. R.

Second Reading Philippians 3:20,21;4:1
This reading is from one of the letters of St. Paul. Jesus promises to come back again, as the king of the world.

Dear friends,
We are all waiting for Jesus to come back again
from his Father in heaven.
When he does, he will make everything different!
He will make us just like himself!
So do not give up.
Keep on doing what Jesus told you to do.
The Word of the Lord.

Gospel Acclamation
There was a sign, nailed to the cross of Jesus,
and it said, "This is the king of the Jews."

Gospel Luke 23:33,34,35,38-43,46
This reading comes from the Gospel of St. Luke.

Jesus died on a cross,
at a place called the Hill of the Skull,
and two thieves were killed with him,
one on either side.
There was a sign nailed to the cross of Jesus

and it said,
"This is the king of the Jews."
So one of the thieves said,
"You're not much of a king, are you!"
But the other thief said,
"Don't say that!
He hasn't done anything wrong."
Then he turned to Jesus and said,
"Don't forget me."
Jesus said,
"I promise you,
I will take you to heaven with me today!"
The Gospel of the Lord.

Prayer of the Faithful

1. For people in God's kingdom, especially everyone in our parish. May we all love and serve God with joy. Lord, hear us. R.

2. For people who have left God's kingdom, especially anyone in our parish. Lord, hear us. R.

3. For the sick people of God's kingdom, especially those in our parish. May they get well and strong. Lord, hear us. R.

4. For the poor and hungry of God's kingdom. May we help them by our prayers. Lord, hear us. R.

5. For those who have gone to God's heavenly kingdom, especially those from our parish. May they be happy forever in heaven. Lord, hear us. R.

Preparation of the Gifts

1. We bring a crown—Jesus is our king.
2. We bring a palm—the palm is for victory.
3. We bring a crucifix—Jesus suffered and died.
4. We bring our lives to God, with the bread and wine.

Second Prayer

God our Father, we bring you our whole lives with these gifts of bread and wine. May we live happily in your kingdom here on earth, by loving and serving you. We ask this through Jesus, your Son, who lives and reigns with you in the unity of the Holy Spirit, one God forever and ever. Amen.

Third Prayer

God our Father, we have come closer to you through meeting Jesus in this Mass. May we go out now to spread the good news of your kingdom. We ask this through Jesus, your Son, who lives and reigns with you in the unity of the Holy Spirit, one God forever and ever. Amen.

Final Blessing

Go in peace, to love God.

46. Easter Sunday

Today is Easter Sunday—the day Jesus rose from the dead. He suffered and died for us, and three days later he rose again.

Penitential Rite
1. You have given us this lovely Easter Day, Lord have mercy.
R. Lord have mercy.
2. You have risen to a new and wonderful life, Christ have mercy.
R. Christ have mercy.
3. May we too may rise to a new life of love, Lord have mercy.
R. Lord have mercy.
May God be good to us, forgive us all that we have done wrong, and one day make us happy with God in our home in heaven.

First Prayer
God our Father, you raised Jesus from the dead to a new life. Help us to rise to a new life of love. We ask this through Jesus, your Son, who lives and reigns with you in the unity of the Holy Spirit, one God forever and ever. Amen.

First Reading Sirach 11:8-10
This reading is from the Book of the Preacher. It tells us that the followers of Jesus shouldn't be glum. We should always be happy, and especially today.

It is wonderful to see the brightness of the sunshine.
It is good to enjoy ourselves
all through our lives,
and especially when we are young.
There's so much to see and do!
May you always be healthy!
May your never be sad!
The Word of the Lord.

Responsorial Psalm Psalm 117
RESPONSE: Alleluia! Alleluia!
1. O praise the Lord all you nations;
Praise the Lord, all you people. R.
2. Praise the Lord,
for the Lord's merciful kindness is great toward us. R.
3. Praise the Lord.
And the truth of the Lord endures forever. R.

Second Reading Ephesians 1:20,21,22
This reading is from one of the letters of St. Paul. It tells us that Jesus died but is alive again now.

Dear friends,
Jesus died—he was killed! But God the Father has raised him to life again.
He has made Jesus the king of the world,
and put him in charge of everything.
He has made him greater than everybody else.
The Word of the Lord.

Gospel Acclamation
Alleluia! Alleluia!
Jesus Christ was dead
and now he is alive.
Let us celebrate the feast of the Lord.
Alleluia! Alleluia!

Gospel Mark 16:2-8
This reading is from the Gospel of St. Mark.

On Sunday morning, very early, just as the sun was beginning to shine, Mary Magdalene, Salome, and Mary, the mother of James, went to the cave where Jesus was buried. When they got there, they found the great boulder had been rolled away from the door. When they went inside, they found a young man there, dressed all in white. At first they were afraid when they saw him, but he said, "Don't be frightened! You want Jesus who was killed, don't you? Well, you can see where they put him, but he's not here now. He is alive! Go and tell Peter and the others that they will see him in Galilee." The women came out of the cave, but they were so frightened that they ran away as fast as they could without saying a word to anybody!

The Gospel of the Lord.

Prayer of the Faithful

As we gather here today to celebrate this great feast of Easter, we pray that people everywhere may feel the presence of the Risen Christ in their lives.

1. We pray for everyone in our parish, especially those we know and love. May they have a happy Easter. Lord, hear us. R.

2. We pray for everyone here. May we show our love as Jesus has shown his. Lord, hear us. R.

3. We pray for our families and friends. May they be filled with peace and love on this happy day. Lord, hear us. R.

4. We pray for the sick and all those in the hospital. Fill them with your hope and love on this Easter Day. Lord, hear us. R.

5. We pray for children everywhere. Help them to grow in your love this Easter time. Lord, hear us. R.

6. We pray for the helpless and the needy. Help us to love and care for them more and more. Lord, hear us. R.

Preparation of the Gifts

1. We bring an Easter egg. Jesus rose from the tomb to a new life.

2. We bring a flower. The new life of the risen Christ is beautiful, perfect, and full of goodness.

3. We bring new clothes. We begin a new life of love.

4. We bring our lives to God, with the bread and wine.

Second Prayer

God our Father, bless these gifts which we, your loving family, bring to you on this lovely Easter Day. We ask this through Jesus, your Son, who lives and reigns with you in the unity of the Holy Spirit, one God forever and ever. Amen.

Third Prayer

God our Father, we have come close to Jesus in holy communion. Help us to stay close to him always. We ask this through Jesus, your Son, who lives and reigns with you, in the unity of the Holy Spirit, one God forever and ever. Amen.

Final Blessing

Go in peace, to love God.

47. Ascension of the Lord

Jesus was going home. He was leaving his friends behind. On Ascension Day, they felt sad as Jesus went up to heaven.Afterward, they were no longer sad but full of joy.

First Prayer
God our Father, make us all joyful on this Ascension Day of Jesus. Help us to follow him, and one day share forever the happiness of heaven. We make this prayer through Jesus Christ, your Son, who lives and reigns with you in the unity of the Holy Spirit, one God forever and ever. Amen.

First Reading Acts 1:13-14
When Jesus left his friends, they spent their time together, praying, waiting.

After the Ascension, the friends of Jesus went back to the city, and stayed in the room where they lived. All the friends of Jesus were there, Peter, John, James and Andrew, Philip, Thomas and Bartholomew, and Matthew, James, Simon, and Jude. And the women who were friends of Jesus were there as well—and his mother, Mary. And they spent their time praying.
The Word of the Lord.

Responsorial Psalm Psalm 46:2, 3, 6, 8
This is a song about the greatness of God, the King of all the earth.
RESPONSE: Clap your hands and shout for joy.
1. Clap your hands and shout for joy, God is the King of all the earth! R.
2. Play the trumpet loud and clear, God is King of all the earth! R.
3. Sing and praise God everyone, God is King of all the earth! R.
4. Praise God now with all your skill, God is King of all the earth! R.

Gospel Acclamation
Alleluia, alleluia.
Jesus said: Go, help everybody everywhere to follow me.
I shall be with you always; Yes, to the end of time.
Alleluia.

Gospel Luke 24:50-53
This is the story of the last time Jesus was seen by his friends.

Jesus took his friends to Mount Olivet outside Jerusalem, and he gave them his blessing there. Then he went away back to his Father, and they didn't see him any more. His friends went back to Jerusalem. But they were no longer sad. They were full of joy.
The Gospel of the Lord.

Prayer of the Faithful
God our Father, we come to you today, with hands lifted up in prayer. We ask you to stay with us always, and help us to bring your Good News to everybody.
1. We pray for everybody in our parish. Help us to show concern and love for each other. Lord, hear us. R.
2. We pray for all the children in our schools. Help us to be friends together, and to help each other. Lord, hear us. R.
3. We pray for all our families. Help us to be kind and good to each other, and to listen to our parents. Lord, hear us. R.
4. We pray for our parents. Help them, as they do their best for us, and lead us to you by word and deed. Lord, hear us. R.
5. We pray for people in need. Help us to notice, and to do all we can, to bring them comfort and peace. Lord, hear us. R.

Preparation of the Gifts
1. We bring a candle. Jesus is with us forever, as he promised on Ascension Day.
2. We bring a Bible. Jesus told us, to spread the Good News to everybody, everywhere.
3. We bring our lives to God, with the bread and wine.

Second Prayer

God our Father, as we celebrate the Ascension of Jesus today, we bring you our gifts. May our gifts help us to rise with Jesus one day, to the joys of heaven. We make this prayer through Jesus Christ, your Son, who lives and reigns with you in the unity of the Holy Spirit, one God forever and ever. Amen.

Third Prayer

God our Father, you have given us Jesus to be with us now, in a special way. Help us always to follow him, with love in our hearts. We make this prayer through Jesus Christ, your Son, who lives and reigns with you in the unity of the Holy Spirit, one God forever and ever. Amen.

Final Blessing

Go in peace, to love and serve the Lord, in gladness and with joy.

48. End of School Year

Today we come together to celebrate the school year. We thank God for our school and our friends. We thank God for showing us such goodness and love through the caring teachers we had this year.

First Prayer
God our Father, we gather together today to thank you for this school year. Thank you for your love, and your goodness to all of us. We make this prayer through Jesus Christ, your Son, who lives and reigns with you in the unity of the Holy Spirit, one God forever and ever. Amen.

First Reading Isaiah 12:4-6
The reading is a song of joy because God is so wonderful.

I want to tell the whole wide world—"God has been good to me!"
I want to tell the whole wide world—"God is wonderful!"
I want to sing and to shout because I am so happy, for God has come to me and God is great!
The Word of the Lord.

Responsorial Psalm Psalm 15:7-9
This is a song of praise and trust in God; God is always there beside us.
RESPONSE: We praise you, Lord.
1. We praise the Lord for the Lord guides us along the right path. R.
2. By day and by night the Lord shows us what to do. R.
3. We shall not fall down if the Lord is there beside us. R.
4. Lord, we are happy for we are safe with you. R.

Second Reading 1 John 3:1, 4, 7, 8
St. John tells us that God is our Father who loves and cares for each one of us.
Dear friends,
See how much God thinks of us—God calls us God's children and

we really are, you know. God takes care of us, so we must take care of each other. God loves us, so we must love each other. If we don't know that, we don't know anything about God our Father, because "God is Love."
The Word of the Lord.

Gospel Acclamation
Alleluia, alleluia.
I want you to be my friends, said Jesus
Alleluia.

Gospel John 15:11, 12, 14. 17
Jesus wants us to love each other, and to be his friends.

"In talking to you as I have done," said Jesus, "I have one aim in view: I wanted you to know the happiness I know. I don't want anything to spoil your happiness. This is the secret of it—my secret, your secret: Love one another as I have loved you. You are real friends of mine—if you do what I have told you. This then is my order: Love one another."
The Gospel of the Lord.

Prayer of the Faithful
God our Father, we thank you for looking after us, through all the people we have come to know this year. We thank them for making our school a happy place, and we ask you to bless them.
1. Bless our school chaplain for the interest shown in our school this year, and for the genuine concern shown to us all. Lord, hear us. R.
2. Bless our teachers for their patience and gentleness, in teaching and helping us this year. Lord, hear us. R.
3. Bless our school secretary for her generous commitment to the school. Lord, hear us. R.
4. Bless our school cleaners for keeping the school clean and spotless. Lord, hear us. R.

5. Bless our caretaker for the important work he does, for the pride he takes in it. Lord, hear us. R.

6. Bless our mothers and fathers for their constant love and care, and for getting us up early and ready for school each day, throughout the school year. Lord, hear us. R.

Preparation of the Gifts

1. We bring seeds. We have been growing together.
2. We bring books and our best work. We have been learning together.
3. We bring a Bible. We have been praying together.
4. We bring a ball. We have been playing together.
5. We bring our lives to God, with the bread and wine.

Second Prayer

God our Father, we bring our gifts and our thanks, for all the good times we had, during this school year. May we all continue to grow in your love. We make this prayer through Jesus Christ, your Son, who lives and reigns with you in the unity of the Holy Spirit, one God forever and ever. Amen.

Communion Litany

RESPONSE: Thank you, Lord.

1. For our thoughtful and helpful school friends. R.
2. For our patient and friendly teachers. R.
3. For the happy times we had together in our classrooms. R.
4. For the games and fun we had on the playground. R.
5. For the new things we learned this year. R.
6. For the days when things were not so good, and we were not so happy. R.
7. For all the people in the school, who were kind to us. R.
8. For our mothers and fathers, who loved and cared for us, all this year. R.

Third Prayer

God our Father, we pray that Jesus, who is with us now, will stay with us as we grow in his love and as we bring his love to others, during the summer holidays. We make this prayer through Jesus Christ, your Son, who lives and reigns with you in the unity of the Holy Spirit, one God forever and ever. Amen.

Final Blessing

Go in peace, to love and thank God.

49. Harvest Time

Today we praise and thank God for all God's gifts, especially the gifts of harvest time.

First Prayer
God our Father, we praise and thank you for your wonderful gifts. We thank you, especially at this time of year, for your gifts of fruit, vegetables, and wheat. We make this prayer through Jesus Christ, your Son, who lives and reigns with you in the unity of the Holy Spirit, one God forever and ever. Amen.

First Reading Leviticus 26:3-5.
A reading from a Book of Moses, telling us that God always sees to the harvest and this makes everyone happy.

God said:
If you obey my rules and do what I ask you to do, then I will give you all the rain you need, just at the right time to make things grow. Everything will grow beautifully in the soil and the trees will be covered with fruit. You will be able to harvest your food all the year round and eat as much as you want.
The Word of the Lord.

Responsorial Psalm Psalm 64:10-14
We give thanks to God for God's many blessings in making this world of ours alive.
RESPONSE: God, you are great and good.
1. You are the one who sends down the early rain to prepare the soil for the seeds. R.
2. You are the one who gathers rain into the rivers to carry water to the crops. R.

---

3. You are the one who gives us gentle showers to soak into the hard, ploughed fields to soften the earth and make the plants sprout and grow. R.

4. You are the one who gives us the harvest filling the valley with golden wheat and fattening the sheep on the green hillsides. R.

5. Let everyone give thanks to you for all your many blessings, and sing for joy. R.

Second Reading

Here Paul is urging us to share what we have together, especially with those who are in need.

Dear friends,

What God wants is that we share what we have together. If we've got more than we really need now and others are in need, we must help them; but sometimes it will be the other way around. God's will is, as I have said, that we shall share what God has given us—and share alike.

The Word of the Lord.

Gospel Acclamation

Alleluia, alleluia.
God said:
Let plants grow in the soil and let there be fruit trees.
Alleluia.

Gospel John 4:35-36

Jesus reminds us that harvest time is wonderful and makes us all happy.

One day Jesus said:

Everything is going just right! There's going to be a marvelous harvest. Isn't it wonderful! One man sows the seeds and three months later the field is full of golden corn, ready for the harvest. Then another man comes and cuts down the corn and stores it in barns. And everyone is happy together.

The Gospel of the Lord.

Prayer of the Faithful

God our Father, you give us harvest time with all its goodness and plenty. Today we pray for those who help to make harvest time possible for all of us.

1. For those who scatter the seed, and sow in the springtime, Lord, hear us. R.

2. For those who tend and care for the crops, as they grow, Lord, hear us. R.

3. For those who are hungry and without food, that we may show them our care, Lord, hear us. R.

4. For those who have plenty while others have none—that we may learn to share, Lord, hear us. R.

Preparation of the Gifts

1. We bring wheat. We thank God for the gift of corn.

2. We bring potatoes. We thank God for the gift of vegetables.

3. We bring apples. We thank God for the gift of fruit.

4. We bring our lives to God, with the bread and wine.

Second Prayer

God our Father, with the gifts of bread and wine, we give you these gifts of the harvest, and all that we are. Unite us all with Jesus and his love. We ask this through Jesus, your Son, who lives and reigns with you in the unity of the Holy Spirit, one God for ever and ever. Amen.

Litany of Thanks

RESPONSE: We praise you, Lord.

1. For the gift of ears of wheat, golden oats, and bearded barley. R.

2. For the gift of sweet juicy apples—red, green, and yellow. R.

3. For the gift of autumn fruits—soft, ripe pears, red and purple plums. R.

4. For the gift of nuts, fruits, and berries of the hedgerow. R.

5. For the gift of fresh vegetable crops. R.

6. For the gift of colorful, bright flowers. R.

Third Prayer

God our Father, you have brought us joy, giving us Jesus in this holy communion. May we bring joy to others, and learn to share the good things of the harvest with each other. We make this prayer through Jesus Christ, your Son, who lives and reigns with you in the unity of the Holy Spirit, one God forever and ever. Amen.

Final Blessing

Go in peace, to love God and to share God's good gifts.

50. Christ the King

The theme of this Mass is Christ the King. Christ is our king, and he is king of the world. We live in his kingdom and we are his loyal children. Today we renew our love and our loyalty to Christ the king.

First Prayer
God our Father, you have given us your Son, to be our Lord and king. Help us to be followers in his kingdom. We ask this through Jesus, your Son, who lives and reigns with you in the unity of the Holy Spirit, one God forever and ever. Amen.

First Reading Isaiah 9:1-2, 6-7
This reading is from the book of a wise man called Isaiah. He is saying that God the Father would send us Jesus to be our king.

Once upon a time,
everyone lived in the dark
but now we can see!
They used to live in a world
that was full of shadows
but now we have a light
to light up our way!
We have God with us
and God has made us happy.
God has sent us a child
who is to be our king
and he will keep everyone safe.
The Word of the Lord.

Responsorial Psalm Psalm 46:2-3, 6. 8
This is a poem from the Book of Praise. We praise the greatness of the king of all the earth.
RESPONSE: The Lord is king of the whole wide world.
1. Clap your hands and shout for joy. R.

2. Play the trumpet loud and clear. R.

3. Sing and praise God, everyone! R.

4. Praise God now with all your skills. R.

Second Reading Ephesians 1:20-22
St. Paul tells us that God the Father has made Jesus king of the world.

Dear friends,

Jesus died—he was killed! But God the Father raised him to life again. He has made Jesus the king of the world, and put him in charge of everything.

In fact, God the Father has made him greater than anybody else.
The Word of the Lord.

Gospel Acclamation
Alleluia, alleluia.
You are the great king that God promised to send us.
Alleluia.

Gospel Mark 8:27-30
When Jesus asked his friends who they thought he was, Peter said that Jesus was the great king that God had promised.

One day Jesus and his friends were walking along the road and he suddenly said, "Who do people think I am?"

His friends said, "Some people think you are John the Baptist! And other people think you are one of the great teachers!"

Then Jesus said, "Who do you think I am?" And Peter said, "You are the great king that God promised to send us."
The Gospel of the Lord.

Prayer of the Faithful
God our Father, we your children, gathered around your table, call to you in prayer. We ask you in faith and love to hear us.

1. We pray for our Pope, our bishops and our priests. May your kingdom come in their hearts. Lord, hear us. R.

2. We pray for our family and for our friends. May your kingdom come in their hearts. Lord, hear us. R.

3. We pray for people who are sad and lonely. May your kingdom come in their hearts. Lord, hear us. R.

4. We pray for people who are sick and weak. May your kingdom come in their hearts. Lord, hear us. R.

5. We pray for our teachers and for those who work for us in school. May your kingdom come in their hearts. Lord, hear us. R.

Preparation of the Gifts
1. We bring a crown. Jesus is our king.
2. We bring our lives to God, with the bread and wine.

Second Prayer
God our Father, we bring you our gifts of bread and wine. We bring with them our joy and loyalty to Christ our king. We make our prayer through Jesus, your Son, who lives and reigns with you in the unity of the Holy Spirit, one God forever and ever. Amen.

Third Prayer
God our Father, Christ our king has come to us. May we take him with us and live happily in his kingdom here on earth. We make our prayer through Jesus, your Son, who lives and reigns with you in the unity of the Holy Spirit, one God forever and ever. Amen.

Final Blessing
Go in peace, to love God.